HANS SONNENBERG

Embracing Adversity

A Life Torn and Rebuilt

HANS SONNENBERG

Contents

Preface

Welcome to the pages of my life. At 82, as I reflect on my journey, I am filled with gratitude and a deep sense of purpose. Life, with its highs and lows, is a beautiful tapestry of experiences that shape us in unimaginable ways.

In 1969, I left Germany for America, driven by a passion for technology and a desire to make my mark. This decision led to a life of unexpected twists and turns. For thirty years, I worked at a large company in Philadelphia, eventually becoming chief information Officer. This role challenged me, taught me perseverance and resilience, and was not without its share of hardships and failures.

Life throws obstacles in our path, testing our resolve and pushing us to our limits. The true measure of character lies not in how many times we fall but in how many times we rise again. I have learned that failure is not the end but a stepping stone to success. Throughout my life, I faced seemingly insurmountable hardships. From living through war to surviving refugee camps, I have had to rebuild my life from nothing more times than I can count. Yet, through it all, I emerged stronger, wiser, and more determined.

Family has always been my anchor, providing strength and a reason to never give up. In these pages, you will witness the power of love, the resilience of the human spirit, and the unwavering support from those who stand by us through thick and thin. As I write my autobiography, I am reminded of the significant events that have shaped my life. Each chapter and experience are pieces of a puzzle that have crafted me into who I am today. My hardships and setbacks have not hindered me—they have propelled me forward.

Acknowledgments

I want to express my deepest gratitude to those who have supported and contributed to my journey. My family and friends played an invaluable role in shaping my life and providing unwavering support throughout the writing process. Their love, encouragement, and belief in me have been my guiding lights.

I extend my heartfelt thanks to Matt DeMazza, a professional editor who has done an exceptional job with *Embracing Adversity*. His expertise and dedication have been instrumental in refining and polishing my work. I am truly grateful for his contributions.

I would also like to express my sincere appreciation to Rachel Merritt for her outstanding cover design. Her wealth of knowledge in design and her assistance in republishing my book on Amazon have been invaluable. Rachel's creativity and professionalism have significantly enhanced the visual appeal of *Embracing Adversity*.

To my readers:

I am truly humbled and grateful to everyone who has taken the time to read my story. Your interest in my life and the lessons I have learned mean the world to me. I sincerely hope that my experiences, both the triumphs and the tribulations, resonate with you and inspire you to navigate your path with courage and resilience.

About the author:

Born in 1941, I witnessed firsthand many tumultuous events that shaped our world. Growing up in East Germany was a challenging experience, but it instilled in me a deep appreciation for freedom and pursuing dreams. After escaping to West Germany, I pursued my passion for computer science, laying the foundation for a successful career.

I took a risk to pursue the American Dream and immigrated to America in 1969. As Chief Information Officer of a prominent company, I dedicated most of my working years to the ever-evolving world of technology. At 52, I retired early and pursued a fulfilling and adventurous life.

Contact Information:

I welcome further engagement and would love to connect with you. Reach out to me through the following channels:

Email: Hans@EmbracingAdversityJourney.com
    Facebook: hans.sonnenberg
    Website: http://EmbracingAdversityJourney.com

Thank you once again for being a part of my journey. Your support means everything to me.

1

A World on the Brink

I was born in 1941 in a small town called Swinemünde, nestled in the heart of Pommern, Germany. Little did I know then, as an innocent child entering this tumultuous world, that the harrowing events unfolding around me would forever shape my life.

In those early years, Swinemünde was a place of beauty and despair. The winds whispered the secrets of a world at war, and the ground trembled beneath the weight of uncertainty.

My father, a brave German soldier, was called to fight on the front lines, leaving my mother to bear the weight of raising four young children alone. We saw very little of him as the days turned into weeks and the weeks into months. His absence was a void in our hearts, which longed for his return.

My mother, a pillar of strength in adversity, fought to provide for us during times of scarcity. Times were tough, and resources were scarce. We had little to eat, but she did her best to nourish our bodies and souls with whatever she could find.

But even as my mother fought to keep our family afloat, a storm was brewing on the horizon. The Russian forces were advancing, their relentless push threatening to engulf our town and its inhabitants. Bombs fell from the heavens, shattering the calm and casting a shadow of fear over our lives.

Day and night, the cacophony of explosions echoed in our ears, a haunting symphony of destruction that left no corner of Swinemünde untouched. The chaos of war had wreaked havoc on the once-calm streets, hiding the familiar landmarks.

And then, one fateful day, the Russian army arrived, their presence an ominous cloud hanging over our town. Swinemünde, once a place of comfort and familiarity, was now under the control of an occupying force. Our lives took on an extra dimension, one where uncertainty reigned supreme and survival became our sole focus.

As I look back on those years, I am reminded of the resilience of the human spirit. Faced with adversity, we clung to hope, our determination burning brightly within our hearts. It is this spirit that carried me through the darkest of times, and it is this spirit that I now seek to capture within the pages of my biography.

I, a witness to the tumultuous events that shaped a generation, must share my story. It is a tale of loss and survival, love and sacrifice, and the indomitable human spirit that refuses to be extinguished. So, let us embark on this journey together as I recount the chapters of my life and the extraordinary world that shaped me.

2

Survival

As the dark clouds of war loomed over Germany, my family found us caught amid chaos. It was 1943, and I was a curious two-year-old boy. I had no clue that the Russian Army's arrival would forever change our lives.

During those chaotic periods, every day was a fight to stay alive. My mother, a strong-willed woman with a compassionate nature, supported our family. She fearlessly and immediately took on a job under General Ivanov, a high-ranking officer from Russia. She made the desperate decision to feed her children, who were starving. But the price she paid was immense. They never paid her a single penny, but offered her food tokens to sustain her family. It was a harsh reality that we had to accept in order to survive.

We were a large family. My sister Karla, the eldest, came into this world in January 1938. Just a year later, my brother Peter arrived in October, and then there was me, Jochen (Hans), born in May 1941, just as the flames of war were consuming the world. We were close-knit, relying on each other for strength and support.

But life can be cruel, and tragedy struck us with a devastating blow. Our youngest sibling, Sabine, was born in November 1942. She was a delicate soul, and fate dealt her a cruel hand. Stricken with diphtheria, there was no cure available. We watched helplessly as she suffered, her tiny body fighting a losing battle. It was heart-wrenching to witness the pain and agony she endured.

When Sabine finally succumbed to the illness at age two, our grief was overwhelming. We knew we had to lay her to rest, but the circumstances were far from ideal. The frozen ground harshly reminded us of the bitter winter surrounding us. In the depths of the forest, we found solace, laying her to rest in a makeshift grave. A simple wooden cross marked the spot, symbolizing our love and loss.

As time passed, we struggled to survive. With our mother occupied with work, much responsibility fell on Karla's young shoulders. She became our caregiver and our compass in a world where darkness reigned. It was a heavy burden for a child, but she did it without complaint.

Every morning, my mother woke up before dawn, her footsteps echoing through the quiet house as she prepared for the day ahead. I was awestruck and fascinated by her unwavering resolve. I often tried to mimic her actions, clumsily attempting to put on my tiny shoes or button my shirt.

As the sun rose over the city, my mother would set off on her daily journey to General Ivanov's office. I bundled up in layers of warm clothing and would wave goodbye from the window, my small hand pressed against the glass. We would then spend our days exploring the neighborhood, our imagination running wild amid the ruins and remnants of war.

One day, Peter, Karla, and I ventured farther than usual; we stumbled upon a group of Russian soldiers huddled around a makeshift fire. Their faces were weathered, their uniforms worn, but their eyes sparkled with hope. We approached them cautiously, our tiny footsteps crunching on the snow-covered ground.

Initially surprised by the sight of three young children, the soldiers soon found themselves enchanted by our infectious laughter and playful antics. They shared stories of their homeland, distant families they longed to see again, and dreams for a peaceful future. I, too young to understand the complexities of war, reveled in the attention and the newfound friendships we had formed.

The bond between us and the soldiers grew stronger as the months passed. They became our protectors and our companions in this uncertain world. We would play games together, have them teach us songs from their homeland, and even share their rations, ensuring we never went hungry. In return, we would bring them small trinkets we found during our explorations, treasures that held little value but meant the world to these soldiers far from home.

The soldiers often took us on their rounds, introducing us to the people they encountered. We would bring smiles to the faces of weary civilians, our presence a reminder that life could still be joyful, even in the darkest times.

One day, as the war ended, General Ivanov called for a celebration. The city of Schwerin was finally free from the clutches of war, and it was time to rejoice. The streets were adorned with colorful banners, and the air was filled with laughter and music. As a three-year-old, I stood on a makeshift stage, surrounded by the soldiers who had become my family.

General Ivanov stepped forward as the crowd cheered, his voice booming through the square. He spoke of the people's resilience and unwavering spirit in the face of adversity. And then, with a twinkle in his eye, he turned to me and declared me an honorary soldier of the Russian Army, a symbol of hope and resilience.

I often wonder where Sabine's final resting place lies. I long to visit her grave and pay my respects to the sister I barely knew. But time has a way of erasing even the most heartfelt memorials. The little wooden cross that once stood tall has succumbed to the passage of time, leaving us without a physical connection to our lost sibling.

Yet Sabine lives on in our hearts, her memory forever in our minds. We carry her with us, a constant reminder of life's fragility and our family's strength. And though the pain of her loss still lingers, we find solace in the bonds we share, knowing that together, we can endure anything life throws our way.

3

The Unyielding Battle for Survival

After the devastating loss of my beloved sister Sabine in the harsh winter of 1945 and with the relentless advance of the Russian Army deep into Germany, my courageous mother made the audacious decision to flee Swinemünde. Determined to find safety, we embarked on a treacherous journey through Poland, venturing toward Germany.

The roads were extremely treacherous, sometimes impassable by the unforgiving winter conditions. Undeterred by the daunting obstacles, my resilient mother devised a plan. She loaded our wagon with its sturdy wooden-spoke wheels and an ample supply of blankets and food, ensuring we had the essentials for our perilous expedition.

With the biting cold gnawing at our bones, we braved the frozen landscapes of Poland, trudging onward through the snow-laden terrain. To shield ourselves from prying eyes, my resourceful mother draped the wagon and our weary bodies in white bedsheets, camouflaging us from the ground and air. We were determined to evade the watchful gaze of soldiers and traverse this treacherous path undetected.

Exhausted, we finally reached the border dividing Germany and Poland. Yet, little did we know, this was merely the commencement of our relentless struggle for survival. The hardships that awaited us within Germany's borders would push our resilience and fortitude to their very limits.

As we crossed into Germany, relief and trepidation washed over us. The war-torn nation stood as a constant reminder of the chaos and uncertainty that consumed the world around us. The battle to survive had only begun, and the path ahead was fraught with danger and hardship.

With unwavering determination, we braced ourselves for the arduous challenges ahead. Each step forward was a testament to our indomitable spirit as we fought to protect our family and forge a future amid the ashes of war. This chapter in our lives would become a testament to the strength and resilience of the human spirit.

The journey through Poland was just the prologue to our harrowing tale, setting the stage for the unimaginable struggles that awaited us within the confines of war-stricken Germany. But with love, courage, and unwavering resolve, we were prepared to face whatever hardships lay in our path as we fought tooth and nail for survival.

4

A Journey of Fear, Uncertainty, and Scarcity

Title: Battling Through the Rubble: Finding Refuge in Rostock

After enduring a treacherous and harrowing journey spanning vast distances on foot, horse and buggy, trains, and rickety trucks, we finally set foot in Rostock in early 1946. This city, the birthplace of my father and home to our relatives, became our sanctuary in the aftermath of relentless bombings by Allied forces.

The once-vibrant and thriving city lay in ruins, its streets scarred by the devastating impact of war. The bombings had left indelible marks, not just on the physical landscape but also on the hearts and minds of its inhabitants. As a young boy, I was thrust into a world of desolation, where fear and uncertainty reigned supreme.

Living in such circumstances was an immense challenge, a constant battle against the terrors that lurked around every corner. The remnants of shattered buildings served as a haunting reminder of the lives lost and the hardships endured. We faced a daily struggle to survive and find solace amid the chaos.

Once a symbol of progress and prosperity, the city's infrastructure lay in ruins. Homes, schools, and public buildings had been reduced to rubble. Necessities became luxuries we could only dream of. Only a select few were lucky enough to have access to food, water, and electricity, while the rest of us had to live in a world of scarcity.

Under the iron grip of military control, our lives became a relentless cycle of fear and unpredictability. We clung to the hope of a brighter tomorrow, even as darkness loomed over us. Yet amid the chaos, we were blessed with the embrace of our relatives, who welcomed us with open arms.

Their kindness and compassion were a beacon of light in our darkest hours. Together, we faced the trials that lay ahead, finding solace in our shared strength and determination. We discovered the resilience of the human spirit, rising above the ruins to rebuild our lives and forge a path toward a better future.

We stayed in Rostock until the summer of 1947, and at the tender age of six, I was already facing the profound challenges that came with the aftermath of World War II. The town was slowly recovering, yet remnants of the war's devastation were still evident. Life was far from easy, especially for a young boy like me. In the prevailing poverty and displacement that lingered, I found myself navigating a world that the war had profoundly shaped. As I ventured beyond the confines of my home and explored the streets of Rostock, the presence of Allied forces cast a palpable weight on my young shoulders. Germany was occupied, and military checkpoints and restrictions on movement were a constant reminder of this new reality. In my daily life, I encountered foreign soldiers, their uniforms a stark contrast to the familiar faces of my community. Yet, through it all, an unwavering spirit of resilience permeated the air. Like countless others across the war-torn world, the people of Rostock refused to succumb to despair. Instead, they found strength in unity, coming together to rebuild their lives and forge a brighter future. I learned to adapt, find solace in the simplest of joys, and embrace the community's power. In the chaotic aftermath of the war, I discovered the true meaning of resilience.

5

The Resilient Spirit as a Young Child in Postwar Germany

As a young child in the war-torn city of Rostock, Germany, I found solace amid the chaos surrounding me. At age four, I possessed a spirit of resilience that would shape my childhood and leave an indelible mark on my future.

I would often venture outside, drawn to the remnants of the bombed houses that littered the streets. The rubble served as my playground, a treasure trove of hidden wonders waiting to be discovered. As I climbed the mounds of debris, my heart raced with excitement, for I knew that within the ruins lay stories of the past.

With each step, I felt the weight of history on my tiny shoulders. Even at such a young age, I understood that the items I found were more than mere trinkets. They were fragments of lives shattered by war, remnants of a time when laughter and joy filled the air.

I found solace in the company of other children. Together, we formed a bond that transcended the hardships we faced. In a world where scarcity reigned supreme, we turned everyday objects into treasures of immeasurable value.

My friends and I would gather in a secret hideout we'd built among the ruins. With our imaginations running wild, we transformed our surroundings into endless possibilities. The broken walls became the walls of a castle, the fallen beams became bridges to far-off lands, and the dusty remnants of furniture became thrones for our make-believe kingdom.

As we played, I couldn't help but notice the hope in my friends' eyes. Each of them had experienced loss and witnessed the devastating consequences of war. Yet, we refused to succumb to despair. Instead, we embraced the power of collective imagination, finding joy in even the direst circumstances.

In this world of make-believe, I discovered the true essence of childhood. Unfettered by the weight of the past, I learned to live in the present, cherishing every moment I spent with my friends. We laughed, played, and created memories forever etched in our hearts.

Reflecting on those days, I understand how deeply they influenced my life. This resilience I cultivated as a child would accompany me throughout my journey, shaping me into the person I would become. I learned to find beauty among destruction, to turn scarcity into abundance, and to cherish the bonds of friendship, even in the darkest times.

Reflecting on my childhood, I am grateful for the indomitable spirit that carried me through those difficult years. The memories of playing alone and with friends in the ruins of Rostock serve as a testament to the human capacity for persistence and the enduring power of imagination. Through it all, I discovered that there is always hope and a reason to play, even in the face of adversity.

6

Family Detained in Rostock

In the quiet town of Rostock, Germany, the year was 1945, and the winds of war were subsiding. However, a knock on our relatives' door was about to shatter my four-year-old innocence.

Bang, bang, bang!

The sound echoed through the house, sending shivers down our spines. We all exchanged worried glances, unsure who could pound on the door with such determination. Little did we know our lives were about to change forever.

As the door swung open, two men stood before us, their plain clothes disguising their true intentions. They held a piece of paper in their hands, and the words scrawled upon it, spelling out our family's fate. The newly established secret police in East Germany had issued an arrest warrant. The charge? We had visited relatives without permission.

My mother's eyes widened with fear, but she wasted no time. With a heavy heart, she rushed into action, knowing that every minute counted. She frantically gathered a few belongings, trying to choose only the essentials. We had no idea when—or if—we would return home.

Days passed, and they transported us to a camp in Schwerin, Mecklenburg, East Germany. We experienced uncertainty and trepidation throughout the journey. The unknown loomed like a dark cloud, casting shadows over our hopes and dreams.

Arriving at the camp, an ununiformed guard greeted us. The air was heavy with despair, and quiet resignation had replaced the once-vibrant spirits of the people inside. Families huddled together, seeking solace and comfort in each other's presence.

Life in the camp was a constant struggle. We faced poor living conditions, overcrowded barracks, and scarce resources. Hunger gnawed at our stomachs as rationed meals barely sustained us. We experienced the days blurring into one another, with no meaningful events to mark the passing of time.

Yet, even in the darkest of times, a flicker of hope remained. Families found solace in their shared experiences, forging bonds that would withstand the trials of the camp. Strangers found comfort and support in one another in a world of darkness.

As the days turned into weeks and the weeks into months, our spirits remained unbroken. We clung to the belief that one day, we would be free from the confines of this camp, free to rebuild our lives and reunite with loved ones. We endured the hardships, never losing sight of our dreams and the hope for a better future.

7

Reunited in Hope: A Father's Return

It was a time of uncertainty and division. The division of Germany into four military occupational zones occurred after the devastating effects of World War II. In the east, where we found ourselves encamped, the Soviet Union held sway. The year was 1946, and it seemed like hope was a scarce commodity.

My father had been absent from our lives since May 1942, and as the years passed, our hope of ever seeing him again dwindled. But my mother, a pillar of strength and unwavering faith, refused to accept the possibility of his demise. She clung to the belief that he would return one day, no matter the odds.

In August of that fateful year, the Potsdam Conference solidified the division of Germany, and we found ourselves trapped in Schwerin Mecklenburg. It was a time of desperation as we longed for news of my father's fate. Each passing day was a painful reminder of his absence.

Then, in September, a glimmer of hope pierced through the darkness that enveloped our lives. A military commission summoned us to appear, and our hearts pounded with anticipation and trepidation. What could they possibly want from us?

As we gathered in that room, the tension was palpable. The stern and stoic military officials delivered news that forever altered our lives. My father, against all odds, was alive. He'd been held captive in a remote military prison deep within Siberia.

Tears streamed down our faces as the weight of their words sank in. The impossible had become possible. The man we had longed to see, to hold in our arms again, would soon be released from captivity. We experienced intense emotions, including relief, delight, and disbelief.

In the following weeks, we filled our days with anticipation and preparation. We could hardly contain our excitement as we imagined we would finally be reunited with my father. The long years of separation were about to end, and a new chapter in our lives was about to unfold.

And then, one day, it happened. As the sun dipped below the horizon, casting a golden glow across the land, a weary figure emerged from the shadows. It was my father, his eyes filled with exhaustion and indescribable happiness.

At that moment, time seemed to stand still. We rushed toward and embraced him tightly, as if afraid he might slip away like a dream. The tears flowed freely, mingling with laughter and cries of joy. We were a family once again, whole and complete.

The journey that followed was not without its challenges. The scars of war ran deep, and rebuilding our lives would take time. But we faced those trials with renewed strength and a deep appreciation for the fragility of life.

Our story, a testament to the power of hope and the resilience of the human spirit, reminds us that even in the darkest times, there is always a glimmer of light. My father's return from Siberia, against all odds, taught us the true meaning of perseverance and the strength of family bonds.

So, as we reflect on those tumultuous years, we do so with gratitude and a profound sense of awe. Ultimately, our divided and longing-filled journey brought us to a place of reunion and rekindled hope. We stand as a testament to the human spirit's tenacity, because we share a love that is unbreakable by space and time.

8

A Harsh Reality

The people of Schwerin found themselves imprisoned in a world under Russian occupation following World War II as the Iron Curtain descended upon Germany. From 1946 to 1950, life in East Germany under the watchful eye of the Russian forces was a relentless struggle for survival. Once a staple of life, food became a scarce and precious commodity. The dark cloud of hunger loomed over every household, casting its oppressive shadow. Every meal was a battle, fought for with determination and resourcefulness. The rations provided by the government were never enough, and desperation pushed even the most honest souls toward the black market. As the Soviets tightened their grip on power, they sacrificed the future of young minds on the altar of ideological control. The schools struggled to function under the weight of neglect and indoctrination, becoming mere shadows of their former selves. The oppressive regime suffocated the hopes and aspirations of a generation, leaving them to wither. Trust became a rare commodity in the face of constant surveillance and the ever-present threat of betrayal. People guarded their conversations, veiled their whispers, and fear tainted even the most innocent interactions. Neighbors became strangers, and the walls of silence grew thicker with each passing day.

Despite the bleakness of our existence, the human spirit refused to be extinguished. In this world of shadows, I discovered a glimmer of hope. Perched high in a tree, armed with a stick and a hook, I became an unlikely hunter, snatching fleeting moments of abundance from passing Russian trucks. With each successful raid, a stolen vegetable symbolized resistance and resilience. Day after day, I embarked on this precarious mission, risking everything for a taste of sustenance. The monotony of the routine was broken only by the constant threat of discovery. However, fueled by an unyielding will to survive, I persevered and became a source of inspiration for those seeking a flicker of hope. Through the darkest times, the people of Schwerin found strength in their shared struggle. They endured the weight of scarcity, the denial of education, and the walls of mistrust. In the face of adversity, they clung to their humanity, never surrendering their longing for freedom. In my story, the spirit of resilience found its embodiment, reminding us that even in the shadows, a flicker of hope can ignite a fire that burns bright with determination.

Eerie silence enveloped East Germany during these bleak years. Forced to navigate a life nearly devoid of electricity and reliable news sources, we lived in perpetual darkness, cut off from the world. Yet, amid the oppressive conditions, the indomitable spirit of the people persisted, forming a testament to human resilience. The scarcity of electricity was a harsh reality that dictated our daily lives. With rationing that limited electric power to a mere few hours each day, we learned to adapt to darkness. The absence of light bulbs casting their warm glow left the streets of Schwerin Mecklenburg enveloped in shadows, creating an atmosphere of uncertainty and trepidation. But within those shadows, a sense of unity and solidarity emerged as neighbors united to support one another through the hardships. Without access to reliable radios, the lifeline to the outside world was severed. News was a luxury, censored and controlled by the occupying forces, leaving us isolated and uninformed. The truth became scarce, and rumors roamed freely without verified information. However, this void of knowledge did not extinguish our curiosity or desire for connection. We sought solace in whispered conversations, exchanging tales and anecdotes, piecing together fragments of truth to create a semblance of understanding.

Winter brought its challenges, as the bitter cold swept through the city streets. Without electricity to power heaters, we huddled together for warmth, sharing blankets and stories and finding comfort in the presence of others. The chill penetrated our bones, but our spirit remained unbroken. The biting cold only fueled our determination to persevere and defy the harsh conditions enforced upon us. Closing the gaps in our lives proved to be an arduous task. Necessities were in short supply as the remnants of war still lingered, casting a long shadow over our everyday existence. But resourcefulness became our ally. We learned to improvise, to make do with what little we had. We met the darkness surrounding us with a fierce resolve to find light within ourselves and our community. As shadows danced along the walls, we refused to succumb to despair. We clung to hope, a beacon guiding us through the darkest times. In the face of adversity, our spirit remained unyielding. We forged bonds, fostered resilience, and demonstrated the strength of the human spirit in the face of unimaginable circumstances. In the memoirs of our lives, we etched the story of a community that endured and thrived even in the absence of electricity, radio, and light.

I possessed an imagination as wild as the rolling hills. Each day was an opportunity for adventure and fun, even in adversity. As a curious and imaginative nine-year-old boy, I found solace in the simplicity of my surroundings. My first teacher, Frau Schmidt, became my beacon of inspiration. She believed in the power of knowledge and nurtured my thirst for learning, even under the watchful eyes of the occupying forces. Despite the challenges, Frau Schmidt taught me and my classmates to embrace our individuality, encouraging us to express ourselves creatively and never lose sight of our dreams.

My unwavering spirit and determination carried me through these turbulent times. Despite the uncertainties and hardships of living in Schwerin Mecklenburg, Germany, in 1950, I remained steadfast in pursuing adventure and growth. My imagination grew bolder daily, and I faced the world with newfound courage. Amid the chaos and turmoil, I learned to find beauty in the most unexpected places. The rolling hills, once a backdrop to my adventures, symbolized resilience and strength. Through it all, I held onto the lessons taught by Frau Schmidt, reminding myself never to lose sight of who I am and the dreams that fuel my spirit. Reflecting on those formative years, I am grateful for the experiences that shaped me. The wild imagination of my childhood has remained a constant companion, guiding me through life's challenges and inspiring me to find joy and wonder in the simplest of moments. The journey continues, and I eagerly embrace what lies ahead, armed with the lessons of my past and the boldness of my spirit.

9

Embracing a Harsh Reality

In 1950, as a nine-year-old living in Schwerin, Mecklenburg, East Germany, I experienced a permanent change in my world. This was the year the Soviets handed over control of East Germany to the Socialist Einheits Party (SED), marking the beginning of a new reality. General Secretary Ulbricht rapidly transformed East Germany into an oppressive police state firmly under the control of the Soviet Union. The SED's rule extended for four decades, encompassing every aspect of our lives. This new reality meant constant surveillance, strict censorship, and limited freedoms. Any dissent or opposition faced swift suppression as they monitored our every move. The weight of fear and oppression hung heavily in the air, stifling dreams and aspirations.

Yet, despite the suffocating atmosphere, the indomitable spirit of the people persevered. We found solace in moments of unity, shared experiences of hardship, and hope for a better future. We believed that one day we would witness the crumbling of the walls that confined us and the realization of our dreams. Little did we know that change was on the horizon. The fall of the Berlin Wall in 1989 would shatter this oppressive regime, unleashing a wave of freedom and liberation that would forever reshape our lives. But for now, as a young child growing up in Schwerin, I navigated this new reality, finding strength in the resilience of my fellow East Germans and holding onto the hope for a brighter tomorrow.

A year later, in 1951, the world thrust me into a life I never wished to be a part of. I was introduced to the compulsory youth organization in Schwerin known as JP Young Pioneers. The weight of this unwanted responsibility settled heavily upon my young shoulders, and I couldn't help but feel a sense of apprehension and resistance toward this new chapter of my life.

The organization served as a stepping stone to pave the way for future membership in the Free German Youth and, ultimately, the ruling party, the Socialist Unity Party of Germany. Its purpose was to instill the values of patriotism, socialism, and loyalty to the state in young minds, molding them into obedient citizens who would actively contribute to the socialist cause.

I vividly remember the day when the Young Pioneers initiated me. The crisp autumn air filled with excitement and trepidation as my classmates and I gathered in the assembly hall. Dressed in our blue pioneer uniforms adorned with red neckerchiefs, we awaited our turn to swear the solemn pledge of allegiance to the socialist state.

The activities of JP Young Pioneers encompassed a wide range of endeavors to foster camaraderie, discipline, and a sense of collective responsibility among its members. We frequently engaged in community service initiatives like tidying up our neighborhoods, tending to school gardens, and aiding older adults. These activities were intended to instill a strong work ethic and a sense of duty toward the betterment of society.

Besides community service, the organization organized educational programs to shape young minds. We attended lectures on the history and principles of socialism, took part in cultural events, and engaged in physical activities to promote health and fitness. The state organized sports competitions, camping trips, and even international exchanges to expose us to different cultures and ideologies while closely monitoring us.

Yet, despite the well-intentioned goals of the JP Young Pioneers, I couldn't help but feel a sense of unease. The mandatory nature of our participation left little room for individual choice or dissenting opinions. They expected conformity and met any deviation from the prescribed path with suspicion and the possibility of consequences. The organization carefully curated its activities to ensure the indoctrination of socialist values and loyalty to the state despite their seemingly innocent nature.

Reflecting upon my time at JP Young Pioneers, I recognize the importance of critical thinking and questioning the world around us. While the organization aimed to shape us into model citizens, it inadvertently fueled my curiosity and passion for personal liberty during these formative years, planting seeds of independent thinking that would eventually sprout and flourish in the face of adversity.

In the following chapters, I will recount the experiences and challenges I encountered as a member of the JP Young Pioneers. From moments of camaraderie to internal conflict, these pages will serve as a testament to the complexities and contradictions that permeated my journey through this compulsory organization. Join me as I navigate the intricacies of a world that demanded my allegiance yet failed to extinguish the flickering flame of individuality within.

As a ten-year-old in 1951, I was filled with excitement and uncertainty about what lay ahead. The Young Pioneers, or JP as we fondly call it, is mandatory for children aged six to fourteen, designed to instill loyalty, discipline, and socialist values. My journey as a Young Pioneer began with an induction ceremony, where I was presented with a red neckerchief, the symbol of our unity and commitment to the socialist cause. Wearing it filled me with a sense of pride, as it signified my dedication to the collective well-being of our nation. The Pioneers' Code was our guiding principle, stressing the importance of friendship, honesty, and diligence.

As a Young Pioneer, I was expected to embody these values in everything I did. However, living up to such ideals was not always easy. I grappled with the complexities and contradictions permeating my journey through this organization. Being a Young Pioneer meant striving for academic and extracurricular excellence. The organization encouraged us to excel in school, attend political education classes, and take part in various sports and cultural activities. While this promoted personal growth, it also added pressure to perform consistently at a high level. One of the challenges I faced as a Young Pioneer was the pressure to conform. The collective often sacrificed individuality for the sake of the greater good. We received constant reminders that our actions reflect on ourselves, the organization, and our socialist ideology. This conformity stifled creativity and independent thinking, leaving little room for self-expression.

The socialist propaganda machine profoundly influenced the Young Pioneers. They instilled in us a deep respect for our leaders and a firm belief in the communist worldview. But as I grew older, I questioned the narratives. I observed inconsistencies between what they taught in school and what I saw in everyday life, leaving me torn between blind faith and critical thinking.

Living in East Germany meant living under constant surveillance. The authorities expected the Young Pioneers to report any signs of dissent or anti-socialist behavior, even if it involved their family members. I was torn between loyalty to my family and the state. As I entered my teenage years, I realized the importance of finding my voice within the confines of the Young Pioneers. I challenged the system subtly, engaging in minor acts of resistance. Whether questioning specific policies during political education classes or seeking alternative sources of information, I was determined to keep my individuality amid the collective ideology. And so, my journey as a Young Pioneer ended as my fifteenth birthday approached.

I reflected on the experiences and challenges that shaped me over the previous five years. While the Young Pioneers provided me with valuable lessons in comradeship and discipline, they have also exposed me to the complexities and contradictions of being forced to join an organization. I was determined to carry the lessons I'd learned with me as I moved forward while also blazing my own path in accordance with my beliefs and values.

10

The Day the World Split in Two

How can I describe the overwhelming emotions that surged when I heard the news as an eleven-year old? The border between East and West Germany was closed indefinitely. The reason behind this drastic measure was the mass migration of people from the East to the West. It was a desperate attempt to escape the oppressive regime that had taken hold in the East. The Soviets had tightened their grip, and hope seemed to dwindle daily. As a young boy, I couldn't fully comprehend the magnitude of this decision. All I knew was that our lives were about to change—and change they did.

The border closure brought about a sense of isolation, a feeling of being trapped within our little corner of the world. Suddenly, the familiar faces that once dotted our city began disappearing as families left everything behind and embarked on a treacherous journey to the West. For my siblings and me, the impact was immediate and profound. Our once-lively city transformed into a quiet town, with empty houses and streets devoid of activity; an eerie silence replaced the laughter and playfulness that had filled the air. Our parents, burdened with worry and uncertainty, tried to shield us from the harsh reality beyond our borders. But even as they put on a brave face, we could sense their fear and desperation. Life became a daily struggle, as scarcity and rationing became the norm. Necessities like food and clothing became luxuries, and we had to learn to make do with our little we had.

It was a time of great hardship, but also a time when we discovered the strength and resilience that lay within us. As a community, we supported one another through acts of kindness and generosity, which fostered friendships. We found solace in the simple joys of life, cherishing each moment of laughter and love. In those moments, the world's weight seemed to lift briefly. Looking back, I realize the border closure was a turning point in our lives. It tore families apart, shattered dreams, and tested the limits of our resilience. But it also taught us the value of perseverance and unity as we discovered the strength that adversity can bring. Today, as I recount this chapter of my life, I am grateful for the lessons it taught me. The scars may still linger, but they remind me of the resilience and determination that carried us through those difficult times. The world may have split in two, but it was in those fragments that we discovered our true selves.

Triumph Against Adversity: My Father's Journey to Independence

My hardworking father, who had been earning a livelihood as a truck driver for the government, suddenly found himself without a job. The closure of the border between East and West meant that the long-haul trips to and from West Germany no longer possible. My father lost his government-owned truck and his source of income, so our family faced an uncertain future. Undeterred by this setback, our family rallied around my father, encouraging him to use our savings to purchase a small truck. With determination burning in his eyes, he took our advice to heart and boldly invested in an old vehicle. Though it needed repair, my father's unwavering spirit led him to scour every junkyard for the parts. Six months later, a resounding sound filled our ears as we heard the engine roar to life. Just a month later, my father had fully restored his truck and was ready to embark on a new journey to sustain our family.

The pride that swelled within us was immeasurable. We cheered him on, celebrating his triumph against adversity. My father's unwavering resolve allowed him to take control of his destiny and refuse to let the surrounding circumstances defeat him. His steadfast spirit provided for our family's needs and instilled in me a profound sense of resilience and the belief that we can overcome any obstacle, no matter the odds.

As I stood there gazing at the old truck with its coal-fired engine, I couldn't help but feel a sense of wonder and amazement. What fascinated me most was its unconventional engine, which ran on coal instead of diesel. My dad, with a proud smile on his face, eagerly explained the mechanics to us. He showed us how to clean the fire compartment, carefully removing remnants from previous journeys. Then he would use paper and wood as kindling, creating a bed of embers. Finally, he would disperse coal into the mix, ensuring its even distribution.

After patiently waiting thirty minutes, my father would ignite the kindling, and a gentle flame would dance within the engine. As the heat from the coal gradually increased, pressure and steam levels rose. The harnessed pressure would power the truck's pistons, propelling it forward. It was a mesmerizing sight, and my young mind struggled to comprehend how something as simple as coal could bring such a heavy machine to life.

In my eyes, my father's ability to understand the engine made him a genius. He would explain how the heat from burning coal converted water into steam, creating the pressure for the engine to function. It was a delicate balance of fire, water, and mechanical precision, all orchestrated by my father's hands.

He and I often embarked on journeys together, with the truck roaring beneath us as we ventured through the countryside. The rhythmic chugging of the engine became a melody that echoed in my heart, symbolizing my father's resourcefulness and determination. I marveled at its ability to transform such humble fuel into a powerful force.

But as time went on, advancements in technology brought about the rise of diesel engines, rendering coal-fired engines obsolete. My father's truck, though still functional, became a relic of the past, a nostalgic reminder of a bygone era. Yet, the memories of those coal-fired journeys remain etched in my mind, a testament to the ingenuity and resilience of my father.

In conclusion, the concept of a coal-fired truck engine was a marvel of its time. It relied on the power of burning coal to generate steam and harness pressure, ultimately propelling the truck forward. My father's ability to understand and operate this unique engine showcased his brilliance and resourcefulness. Although the era of coal-fired engines has long passed, the memories of my father's truck will forever hold a special place in my heart, reminding me of a time when coal fueled our journeys and dreams.

11

Transformation of East Germany into a Socialist State

As a young boy of twelve, I witnessed the transformation of our country into a socialist state. The winds of change blew through the streets of Schwerin, East Germany, carrying hope and uncertainty.

One of the most significant changes was the collectivization of agriculture. Large, collective farms where workers toiled together for the greater good replaced the once-familiar sight of individual farms, which both fascinated and perplexed me. Nationalized industries also became a prominent feature of our daily lives. Factories that were once privately owned were under state control, intending to create a more equitable society. Authorities carefully regulated our lives through quotas and directives, ensuring efficient allocation of resources. Sometimes, it felt like we are all part of an elaborate puzzle, with each piece playing a vital role.

A Battle for Nourishment: The Great Chicken Coop

This period is etched deeply in my memory. Empty stores, their barren shelves serving as daily reminders of our hardships, marred the landscape of my existence. Oh, the challenges we faced to secure even the most basic sustenance! Each day, we embarked on a grueling quest to lay our hands on the meager provisions available. But there was a catch: Certain food items were only obtainable on specific days. These elusive opportunities created an atmosphere of anticipation and determination as we strategically planned our lives around these precious windows of availability. Long lines became the arteries of our society, pulsating with a palpable yearning for sustenance. We stood shoulder to shoulder, united by our shared hunger, as the hours trickled away. The camaraderie that formed in these queues was an unintended silver lining, a testament to the resilience of the human spirit. In those moments, we transcended the boundaries imposed upon us and found solace in our collective struggle.

Rationing was a huge part of our daily lives. Our food stamps became precious tokens, emblems of survival that we desperately clung to. Each stamp represented a sliver of hope, a fleeting chance to secure a morsel of nutrition for our families. How we stretched each precious item, ensuring that not a crumb would go to waste! In this tale of deprivation, we must recognize the extraordinary lengths we went to survive.

Allow me to recount a tale from my youth in East Germany from the late 1940s to the mid-1950s. Food was about as rare back then as a unicorn riding a rainbow. But my resourceful father came to the rescue! Picture this: a decrepit old building of discarded materials begging to be repurposed. Well, my father had a brilliant idea. He built an enclosed chicken coop out of junk material. Yep, you read that right, a chicken coop! We gathered a flock of twenty feathered friends, and they became our ticket to survival. In those tough times, bartering was the name of the game. And what better to trade than fresh eggs? We struck up a deal with our neighbors, swapping those golden treasures for other needed goods.

But here's where things get interesting: My mother, bless her soul, was the egg mastermind. She kept meticulous records of each chicken's egg-laying. And get this: She even had a secret technique to figure out who was responsible for each egg—which, I must warn you, is not for the faint of heart! She had a particular finger-stick method that involved, well, you know where. Yes, my friends, she would use her magical finger wand to determine which hen would give us that delightful egg. This way, she could accurately promise the right amount of eggs for trade. Oh, the lengths we went to for survival!

But that's not even the best part of this poultry adventure. My ingenious father rigged a rope system that connected the coop's door to our bedroom. Can you imagine? He could open the door without even leaving his cozy bed! It was like a chicken magic show, until one fateful day when disaster struck. My father's grip on that rope wasn't as firm as he thought. It slipped right through his fingers, and in the blink of an eye, off went a chicken's head! I know it may sound morbid, but as kids, we couldn't help but burst into uncontrollable laughter. It was like an unexpected twist from a slapstick comedy.

So, there you have it, my friends. The incredible saga of The Great Chicken Coop. It is a tale of resilience, resourcefulness, and a touch of absurdity. In those challenging times, we learned to make the most of what we had, even if it meant sticking fingers where they didn't belong and accidentally beheading a chicken or two. Life was never dull!

As I reflected on the changes sweeping through our nation at that time, I couldn't help but feel a mix of emotions. The world around me was developing, and I was witnessing a pivotal moment in history.

12

Forbidden Airwaves

We had limited access to entertainment, and the state tightly controlled what we could listen to or watch. Oh, how I cherished my radio! It was my window to the outside world, through which I could escape from the confines of our small city. The radio was our primary source of information and entertainment, connecting us with the rest of East Germany. We had a few radio stations, each with its own unique programming. During the day, we could tune in to the official station of the German Democratic Republic, the "Deutscher Demokratischer Rundfunk" (DDR). They would broadcast news, political discussions, and educational programs. It was a way for the government to inform us about their policies and achievements. In the evening, DDR would transform into a cultural hub. They would air classical-music concerts, theater performances, and readings of famous literary works. It allowed us to appreciate our rich heritage and connect with the arts. We also had a regional station called "Rundfunk der DDR - Bezirksstudio Schwerin." This station focused on local news, events, and regional cultural programs. It fostered a sense of unity within our community and helped us stay informed about what was happening in our immediate surroundings.

In 1955, we didn't have a television set in our household, but I remember seeing them displayed in shop windows. TV was a luxury that seemed light years away from our grasp. These big, bulky boxes emitted a magical glow, captivating passersby. However, the state strictly regulated television programming. We could not watch Western TV channels, which were deemed ideological threats. The government wanted to shield us from the influence of the capitalist world and preserve our loyalty to the socialist cause. Occasionally, we would hear rumors of people secretly watching these forbidden broadcasts, but such acts were hazardous and could lead to severe consequences if caught. The government had methods to detect illegal antennas or unauthorized connections, and those found guilty of such activities faced imprisonment or other forms of punishment. Though I never had the chance to watch TV during that time, I have heard stories of propaganda-filled shows highlighting the achievements of the socialist regime. They would showcase the advancements in industry and agriculture and the success of the working class. It was a way to reinforce our faith in the socialist ideals and maintain control over the narrative.

These restrictions on our access to Western media may have limited our exposure to different perspectives, but they also unified us. We relied on each other for news, information, and entertainment. We would gather around the radio, discussing the latest programs or eagerly waiting for our favorite shows. Looking back, we felt curious and eager during those days. We yearned for more freedom, choices, and the ability to explore the world beyond our borders. But we also found solace, joy, and connection in the limited options we had.

13

The Hilarious Bathtub Chronicles: An Epic Family Adventure

Let me take you back to the good old days in Schwerin, Mecklenburg in the mid-1950s, when I was just an enthusiastic youngster between the ages of 10 and 15, where having hot water was as almost rare as spotting a unicorn in the wild. In order to begin the daring adventure of taking a bath, we had to gather all our bravery and tap into our inner MacGyvers. Our secret weapon? A colossal kettle in the basement, capable of holding a whopping fifty gallons of water. But there was a catch: It took an eternity to heat! We're talking about at least an hour of anxious anticipation, like waiting for Christmas morning. Once that baby was bubbling and steaming, it was time for the ultimate family teamwork extravaganza. We'd form a chain, passing buckets of this precious liquid gold up the stairs and into our apartment. It was like a synchronized dance routine, except we were hauling buckets instead of making graceful leaps and twirls.

Finally, with the Herculean task complete, the moment of truth arrived. Standing there like a majestic oasis in the desert, the bathtub beckoned us to its watery embrace. But, of course, there was a pecking order. My dear old dad would take the plunge first. Then, my mom would gracefully follow suit, radiating elegance even in the face of lukewarm water. Next in line was my sister, who would tiptoe in like a ballet dancer, trying to avoid the inevitable chill. And let's not forget my naughty brother, who would splash around like a misbehaving dolphin, causing waves of hilarity. Finally, it was my turn. Oh, the anticipation! But alas, by the time I dipped my toe into that tub, the water had transformed into a tepid concoction that resembled something straight out of the sewer system. I'd stand there, contemplating my fate, wondering if my future self would ever experience the joy of a hot, steamy bath. But fear not, my friends, for I had a secret weapon.

I became the master of disguise and the wizard of cleanliness. Armed with a trusty washcloth, I'd perform a theatrical performance worthy of an Oscar-winning actor. I'd pretend to luxuriate in the water's warm embrace while stealthily scrubbing away the grime with my magical washcloth. And that, my dear readers, is the tale of our epic bathtub chronicles. It is a story of triumph over adversity and family unity in the face of a cold-water calamity. It may not have been the most luxurious bathing experience, but it gave us memories to chuckle about for years. So, remember, next time you take a hot shower or soak in a warm bubble bath, spare a thought for those of us who braved the icy waters of the socialist state and a brief prayer of gratitude for the wonders of modern plumbing. Cheers to the bathtub warriors forever immortalized in the hilarious annals of our family history!

You see, this marvelous kettle served a dual purpose. Not only did it bathe us in its warm embrace, it served as a wash kettle for our clothes. Our family had quite the system in place for this old-fashioned washing machine. We'd gather 'round, armed with a double bell-shaped metal object mounted on a stick. Oh, the satisfaction of punching that cloth floating in the water! We'd give it a good wallop for about an hour until those garments sparkled like they were fresh out of a fancy boutique.

But wait, there's more! The kettle was also a key player in transforming sugar cane into delectable syrup, a process that was an adventure of its own. Instead of the bell on the stick, we wielded a magnificent S-shaped knife atop our trusty wooden companion. With our mighty knives, we chopped those sugar cane into bits, boiled them, and drained their precious juice. The real magic happened when we started cooking that juice. Oh, the sweet aroma that filled the air! We'd stir that pot for 24 hours, never ceasing our rhythmic dance. And what emerged from that molten concoction? None other than the golden nectar we call molasses, fit for the gods themselves! But we weren't done, oh no! We'd let molasses cook for an extra six hours if we felt adventurous. And what do you think happened? It transformed into pure, heavenly brown, sticky sugar! Can you believe it? We had the power to create sugar right there in our basement! Of course, you must be wondering who carried out these daring feats. Why, it was the kids, of course! We were the brave souls who stood at the forefront of syrup-making innovation, our tiny hands stirring the pots with unwavering determination. We were the unsung heroes of the household, the syrup masters in training.

So, there you have it. The wild adventures of the syrup-making savant. It is a tale of hot water baths, clothes-punching sessions, and the sweet alchemy of transforming sugar cane into liquid gold. It may sound like fiction, but I assure you, every glorious moment was real. And it's a story I'll proudly pass down to future generations, for it is a testament to the joy and creativity of the simplest tasks.

14

Journey through Education: Memoirs of a Young Boy in East Germany

As I sat down to write this memoir, I couldn't help but feel nostalgic while reflecting on my educational journey as a boy in Schwerin, East Germany. Born in 1941, I was fortunate enough to witness a time of significant change and upheaval, all of which left an indelible mark on my education. In 1947, at the tender age of six, I embarked on my compulsory education journey. The educational system in East Germany was characterized by its emphasis on discipline and strict adherence to the ideals of the communist regime. We would line up in neat rows every morning, reciting slogans and singing patriotic songs. In that world, they valued conformity above all else.

My classroom was a microcosm of the society we lived in. Our teacher, Frau Schmidt, was unwavering in the party's ideology. Her stern demeanor and piercing gaze made even the bravest soul quiver. One day, she caught me whispering to my friend Fritz during a history lesson. To make an example out of me, she assigned the entire class a week's worth of extra homework. It was a lesson I would never forget.

Learning extended beyond the walls of our school. Extracurricular activities, from choir rehearsals to sports competitions, were an important part of our education. One particularly memorable event came during the annual sports day, when I tripped over my feet during the sack race, resulting in a tumble that had everyone in stitches. At least I made it into the school's Hall of Fame for the most unforgettable fall!

Education wasn't always a bed of roses. Resources were scarce, and we often had to make do with outdated textbooks and limited materials. Yet, our teachers always ignited the spark of curiosity within us. They taught us resilience and adaptability, molding us into lifelong learners.

Although the educational system was strict, it couldn't suppress the mischievous spirit within us young boys. We often engaged in harmless pranks between classes to lighten the mood—one memorable incident involved swapping our teacher's chalk with painted white sticks. The look of confusion on Frau Schmidt's face as she tried to write on the blackboard with a white stick brings a smile to my face to this day.

Another amusing anecdote took place during a chemistry experiment. Our teacher, Mr. Müller, demonstrated the reaction between vinegar and baking soda. A loud fizzing sound filled the room as he poured the vinegar into the beaker. But instead of fizzing, the mixture exploded, sending vinegar flying across the room and onto poor Mr. Müller's face. We couldn't help but burst into laughter—even Mr. Müller joined in, wiping vinegar off his glasses with a sheepish grin.

But just as my education was reaching its peak, fate threw a curveball. In 1955, my mother hatched a plan for our family to escape to West Germany, leaving behind our unfinished lives in Schwerin. It was a decision that abruptly interrupted my education after eight years, leaving me without a formal graduation. Little did I know then that this escape would shape my life forever.

As I conclude this chapter of my educational journey, I am reminded of the resilience and determination that guided me through those formative years.

Although the path had challenges and unexpected turns, it also had moments of laughter and camaraderie. Join me in the next chapter as I delve into the thrilling tale of our escape to West Germany and in the following chapters as I carve a fresh path for myself in a land of new beginnings.

15

The Great Escape

In 1955, at age fourteen, in the beautiful city of Schwerin, Mecklenburg, I never could have imagined the incredible adventure ahead. It was a time when the Iron Curtain stood tall, dividing our nation and our dreams. The oppressive regime suffocated our spirits, but my brave mother hatched a plan that would change our lives forever.

It was a chilly autumn evening when my mother called us into her room, her eyes filled with determination and a hint of fear. She whispered urgently, "Children, we cannot stay here any longer. We deserve freedom and a life without constant surveillance and limitations. We are going to escape to West Berlin."

My heart raced with excitement and trepidation. Escape? The idea seemed impossible, yet my mother's unwavering resolve gave me hope. She explained various ways to make the arduous journey, but the most popular method was the train to Berlin. I remember that day vividly, as if it happened just yesterday.

We were boarding the train, my heart pounding with anticipation and fear. The controls on the train seemed to grow more intense as we inched closer to Berlin, a palpable tension in the air. My mother, always resourceful and prepared, layered us with extra clothing, ensuring we had enough warmth for the arduous journey ahead. She had also packed two suitcases filled with our meager belongings, carefully strategizing to give us the best chance to escape unnoticed. Two elderly women stepped in and assumed responsibility for the bags. It was a spontaneous act of compassion and bravery, and we were forever grateful.

The police, suspicious but unwilling to delve deeper, questioned us about our travel destination. Thinking quickly, my mother told them a lie—that I was gravely ill and in need of urgent surgery. She mentioned a hospital, the name of which I can only recall as sounding like "Charlitay." It was a desperate attempt to divert their attention and make them believe that our journey to East Berlin was a matter of life or death. As the train rumbled on, my heart heavy with the weight of the lies we had woven, I couldn't help but notice the violence outside. The police were engaged in shooting several people. It was a chilling reminder of the dangers that lay ahead and the risks we were taking to escape the oppressive regime. The journey seemed endless, each passing mile etching deeper into my memory. Berlin, a divided city by fences and ideologies, was the last stop for the train. We stepped off the train, holding our breath, hoping that our carefully crafted story would hold up under scrutiny. Our lives depended on it.

Our next challenge was to discover a method for crossing into West Berlin, a place where dreams could come true. In those days, people used various methods to escape from East Berlin to West Berlin. But one of the most popular ways was by train. The train ride was a nerve-wracking experience, but it offered a glimmer of hope. It was both exhilarating and terrifying. As it chugged along, it passed through all four sectors of Berlin: the British, French, American, and Russian Sectors. I remember the rhythmic clatter of the wheels on the tracks, the sound echoing in my ears like a heartbeat, my anticipation growing.

My siblings and I clung to our mother, our eyes wide with fear and excitement. My heart raced as the train approached West Berlin, the American Sector. I wondered how we would escape and slip through the system's cracks that sought to keep us confined. The heavily guarded border posed an even more uphill task for us, although the Berlin Wall had not yet been erected. Suddenly, the train screeched to a halt. This was our moment, our chance to break free from oppression. The doors hissed open, and many people rushed towards the exit. In that chaotic frenzy, my mother grabbed our hands and pulled us through the crowd, navigating the sea of bodies toward freedom. We followed her lead, weaving through the station, our hearts pounding in sync with each step. The air crackled with anticipation, as if the atmosphere sensed our desire to be free. It was a race against time, a dance with fate. And then, miraculously, we stood on the other side of the border. We had made it. We had crossed into West Berlin, leaving behind the hardships and limitations of the East. A newfound sense of possibility and hope took the weight off our shoulders.

Looking back, I realize our escape was a miracle. It was a testament to our parents, whose bravery defied all odds to give their children a chance at a better life. It was a pivotal moment that shaped the rest of our journey and our story.

My father, a courageous and resourceful man, had devised this daring plan to escape the clutches of the East German regime. Being an independent truck driver, he had developed a network of connections and a reputation for being trustworthy, even in the eyes of the authorities, which would prove invaluable as he navigated the treacherous path toward freedom. Under the watchful eyes of the East German government, my father underwent intense scrutiny and swore allegiance to the regime, concealing his true intentions all the while. Those who held the power to grant him unique papers to cross the heavily guarded border into West Berlin trusted him. And there, like a beacon of hope in the darkness, my father arrived with his truck in West Berlin. The sight of him filled us with a renewed sense of determination and reassurance.

With each passing moment, the distance between us and the confines of East Berlin grew.

In the following years, we would cherish the freedom we had fought to attain. It was freedom that allowed us to dream, to pursue our ambitions, and to shape our destinies. And so, as I reflect upon this meaningful chapter in my life, I am grateful for the bravery and ingenuity of my father and mother, who defied the odds and led us to a life of liberty.

This chapter is a testament to the power of hope, the strength of family, and my unwavering belief in a brighter tomorrow. It is a reminder that no matter the obstacles we face, we can overcome them with steadfast determination and a boldness that refuses to be silenced.

16

Seeking Refuge

After what felt like an eternity, we finally reached the safety of West Berlin. It was a bittersweet moment, as we knew our journey was far from over. Exhausted and hungry, we sought refuge in the bustling streets, blending in among the crowds as we approached the West Berlin Police Station.

The station stood tall and imposing, a beacon of hope among the chaos that engulfed our lives. With trepidation, we entered its doors, ready to present ourselves as refugees needing assistance. The weary faces of my family mirrored my own, each filled with relief and apprehension. We were met with stern faces and probing questions. The officers, though well-intentioned, needed to ensure our legitimacy and protect the safety of those within their borders. We answered every query truthfully, knowing our lives depended on our ability to convince them of our dire circumstances.

Hours turned into an eternity as we were questioned relentlessly. The dimly lit room seemed to close in on us, amplifying the weight of our exhaustion. Yet, we persevered, knowing this was a small sacrifice on our journey to freedom. Finally, the officers seemed satisfied with our responses as the clock struck three in the morning. We were granted a temporary respite, a reprieve from the relentless questioning. With heavy hearts, we bid farewell to the police station, leaving behind the security of its walls for the unknown.

The refugee camp, a converted gymnastic school, became our temporary home. Inside its walls, we found rows of thin mattresses spread across the floor, the meager provisions provided for those seeking refuge. It was a stark reminder of the challenges we had overcome and the trials that still lay ahead. Separated into two halls, one for men and the other for women and children, we settled into our designated space. The air was thick with anticipation as we navigated the unfamiliar dynamics of communal living.

Strangers became companions, bound together by a shared longing for freedom and a yearning for a better future. Those initial nights were challenging. Scared and bewildered, I experienced terrible nightmares that plagued my restless sleep. The weight of anxiety and the flashbacks of our perilous escape to West Berlin combined with the haunting image of lifeless bodies we encountered along the way had a profound effect on my young mind. It was as if those haunting memories were etched into my very being, causing me to struggle to breathe and leaving me filled with an overwhelming sense of dread. Every night, like clockwork, a voice would echo through the camp's speakers at eight o'clock, requesting that all the men and women separate and move into their designated halls. An hour later, darkness would descend, and the lights were dimmed. It was during these moments that my inner demons seemed to grow stronger.

Unable to find solace in sleep, every night became a battle that I fought alone. I would weep myself to sleep, hoping that somehow my tears would wash away the nightmares that plagued me. But as the sun rose, I would wake up, only to find myself trapped within the realm of endless nightmares once again. In this darkness, my mother became my guiding light. She would hold me close, comforting me as best she could until I drifted back into slumber. Her warmth and love were the only things that provided a glimmer of hope amid the despair that surrounded us.

The trauma of those nights continued to haunt me long after we left the refugee camp. The constant fear and anxiety had left an indelible mark on my young soul. For years to come, I struggled with a stutter, my words stumbling over the memories I desperately tried to suppress. But even in the darkest of times, there is always a flicker of hope. Through the love and support of my family and the resilience that grew within me, I slowly overcame the nightmares that had once consumed my nights. Though the scars remained, I learned to carry them with strength and determination. Days turned into weeks, and the routines of camp life became our new reality. We found solace in the companionship of fellow refugees, sharing stories of our pasts and dreams of what lay ahead. Though confining, the walls of the camp became a sanctuary where we could rebuild our shattered lives.

As time passed, our temporary refuge became a testament to perseverance. We held onto the hope that one day, we would leave this makeshift home behind, stepping into a world where freedom was not just a distant dream. With each passing day, we grew stronger, knowing that our escape had been worth every sacrifice. And in the embrace of our fellow refugees, we found a sense of belonging. Our journey was far from over, but with each passing chapter, we grew closer to the freedom we desperately sought.

I will never forget the day my mother, the queen of spontaneity, whisked us away from the mundane life of the refugee camp. With a twinkle in her eye and an impeccable sense of fashion, she ensured our hair was perfectly groomed, and we wore our best clothes. Little did we know that this escapade would take us on a wild journey through the bustling streets of West Berlin. As we strolled hand in hand, my heart pounded with excitement and curiosity. My mother's voice, tinged with a mischievous tone, promised to show us a glimpse of our soon-to-be new life. We rounded the corner and hopped onto a shiny, modern trolley car like celebrities on their way to a red-carpet event. Oh, the stares we received as we took our seats! People couldn't help but be captivated by our impeccable style and undeniable charm.

As the trolley car zoomed through the city, our eyes widened with sheer amazement. Everywhere we looked, there were sights to behold. Beautifully dressed people carried shopping bags filled with treasures. It was as if we had stumbled upon the world's fashion capital, where even the pigeons strutted their feathers with pride. After an eternity of anticipation, we finally arrived at our destination. Stepping out of the trolley car, we crossed the street and entered a grand department store that seemed to stretch into infinity. I couldn't believe my eyes. It was like stepping into Schlaraffen Land, a mythical realm overflowing with milk and honey. We wandered through the store, our jaws dropping at every turn. The clothes gleamed like precious gems, begging to be touched. The shelves were stacked with the latest gadgets and gizmos, each more extravagant than the last. And the salespeople! They greeted us with beaming smiles, eager to assist us in our quest for the perfect ensemble.

While perusing the aisles, my mother's infectious laughter filled the air. She playfully tried on eccentric hats and modeled dresses fit for a queen. I couldn't help but join in the fun, twirling around in oversize sunglasses and strutting my stuff down the imaginary runway of the shoe department. In this whimsical wonderland, the time seemed to stand still. We forgot about the hardships we had endured and the uncertainties that lay ahead. All that mattered in that moment was the pure joy we experienced as we immersed ourselves in this magical escape.

Eventually, reality tugged at our sleeves, reminding us that our adventure had to end. Reluctantly, we returned to the trolley car, our new memories stamped forever in our minds. Our hearts were filled with hope and determination as we returned to the refugee camp. We knew that one day, we would return to this land of milk and honey not as mere visitors but as residents of a brighter future. This day would forever be a reminder that even in the face of adversity, laughter and a touch of whimsy can light the way to a better tomorrow.

A special announcement would blare over the speakers every Monday at the camp like clockwork, filling our hearts with hope and excitement. It was the call we had all been waiting for—the supply truck was coming! Now, let me tell you, this wasn't just any ordinary truck. This magnificent vehicle was our lifeline, our beacon of joy in an uncertain world. It promised something magical: crates of fresh fruit generously donated by big, kindhearted super-markets. How our eyes would light up at the mere thought of those crates overflowing with nature's sweetest gifts. Oranges, apples, and bananas—oh my! These were exotic fruits that I had only ever heard of in tales whispered by fellow camp dwellers. But today, my friends and I would experience their juicy wonder firsthand.

The anticipation was palpable as the truck rumbled into the camp. We all gathered outside, like a colorful mosaic of hope, ready to receive our share of this fruity treasure. I stood there, my heart pounding with excitement, as I extended my hand toward the truck, hoping to glimpse the wonders it held within. And then, it happened. A warm smile greeted me as a kind soul handed me a bag filled with oranges and bananas. I couldn't believe my eyes! These vibrant fruits, so foreign and tantalizing, were now nestled in my very own hands. It was as if a piece of paradise had descended upon us, bringing with it a taste of a world beyond the confines of our camp. What struck me the most, however, was the incredible display of gratitude and orderliness among my fellow refugees. We all patiently waited our turn, cherishing each moment as we received our bags of fruit. It was a sight to behold—a tangible reminder that kindness and appreciation could flourish even in adversity.

The generosity from the outside world touched each one of our hearts. We were reminded that we were not forgotten and that there were people who cared deeply for our well-being. It was a lesson that stayed with me throughout my life, a reminder always to be grateful for the simple joys that come our way.

From that day forward, Mondays held a special place in my heart. It wasn't just about the fruit, you see, but about the joy and unity it brought to our little community. It was a small reminder that there's always room for laughter, uplifting spirits, and a taste of the extraordinary.

17

From Refugee Camps to the Skies

It was a crisp morning when the unexpected letter arrived, bearing news that would forever change the course of my life. After three long weeks of seeking refuge in the overcrowded and chaotic camp in West Berlin, someone informed my family that we would finally be leaving. We could feel the excitement and anticipation as we read the letter, and hope for a brighter future filled our hearts.

We were to be flown to Hanover, a city brimming with possibilities, via the iconic Berlin Tempelhof Airport. The mere thought of soaring through the skies in an airplane was both exhilarating and intimidating. As a young child who had never even ventured beyond the borders of my war-torn homeland, the prospect of this journey ignited an indescribable sense of wonder within me. On the day of our departure, the sun rose with a radiant glow, casting a golden hue upon the bustling refugee camp. The air crackled with electrifying energy as families prepared for the unknown. I clung tightly to my parents' hands, my heart pounding with excitement and trepidation. Little did I know that this flight would not only transport me physically but also symbolize the soaring of my spirit, breaking free from the chains of adversity.

Stepping foot onto the vast tarmac of Berlin Tempelhof Airport, my eyes widened in awe. The sheer magnitude of the aircraft that awaited us was beyond anything I had ever imagined. It stood tall and majestic, its metallic wings spread wide, ready to carry us toward a new beginning. As we boarded the plane, a sense of adventure and hope permeated the air, mingling with our nervousness.

Inside the aircraft, I marveled at the rows of seats, each equipped with tiny windows that framed the world outside. With their impeccable uniforms and warm smiles, the cabin crew welcomed us aboard, easing our fears with their reassuring presence. As the engines roared to life, my anticipation reached its peak. The plane taxied along the runway, its wheels bouncing gently over the uneven surface. And then, with a surge of power, we were airborne.

As we ascended into the clouds, I felt the enveloping sensation of weightlessness, leaving behind the familiar land that had etched itself into my memory. Through the tiny window, I witnessed the sprawling cityscape of Berlin morph into a miniature patchwork of greens and browns, as if nature were bidding us farewell. My gaze shifted skyward, where the endless blue expanse stretched before me, promising a world of boundless opportunities.

As the hours passed, I found solace in the gentle hum of the engines, lulling me into a state of tranquility. I allowed my mind to wander, envisioning the life that awaited us in Hanover. Would the people be kind? Would the new camp provide a sense of stability and belonging? These thoughts swirled within me, mingling with the clouds that brushed against the plane's windows.

Eventually, our descent began, and my heart skipped a beat. The wheels touched the runway with a soft thud, signaling our arrival in Hanover. We disembarked from the plane, our weary bodies infused with newfound vigor. From Hanover Flughafen, we embarked on a bus journey that would take us to our destination, Lage Lippe, nestled in the picturesque landscape of Westphalia.

Lage/Lippe was a small town in the district of Lippe, in North Rhine-

Westphalia, Germany. It was eight kilometers northwest of Detmold, the district's administrative center, with a population of about 27,000 in 1955. The town is near the Teutoburg Forest, where the famous battle between the Romans and the Germanic tribes occurred in 9 AD.

We arrived at yet another makeshift camp in a converted gymnasium. Little did we know that this temporary haven would provide us with a much-needed respite from the hardships we endured in the bustling refugee camp we left behind in Berlin.

As we arrived at the camp, a sight greeted our tired bodies and weary souls, bringing tears of relief to our eyes. We no longer had to endure the cold, bare floors and the cramped spaces we had grown accustomed to.

Oh, the luxury of a bed! It seemed like a dream come true after weeks of sleeping on the unforgiving floor of the Berlin camp. The softness of the mattress cushioned our bodies, allowing us to sink into comfort we had almost forgotten. Understanding the importance of privacy, the camp's management had thoughtfully installed partitions to grant us a semblance of personal space. It was a sanctuary that felt like a palace compared to the stark realities of our recent past.

We have experienced a renewed sense of hope and belonging in the camp. Laughter, conversations, and shared stories of resilience filled the vibrant atmosphere. People from different corners of the world had come together, forming an unconventional family united by circumstance. In this melting pot of cultures, we discovered a newfound appreciation for diversity and the strength it brings when we stand together.

The camp's residents quickly formed a tight-knit community, supporting each other through the challenges ahead. We shared meals, exchanged recipes, and discovered the simple joys of breaking bread together. In the evenings, the camp's makeshift common area transformed into a lively gathering spot where impromptu performances and talent shows provided a much-needed escape from our worries. In these moments, we found solace and laughter, reminding us that even in the darkest times, there is always room for joy.

As the days turned into weeks, we marveled at the camaraderie that blossomed within the camp's makeshift walls. Despite our hardships, the spirit of perseverance was strong among us. We had developed from being mere refugees into a group working together for a better future, hoping to rebuild our lives.

In this unexpected haven, we discovered more than just physical comfort. We learned the true power of compassion, empathy, and the unwavering human spirit. We learned that amid the chaos of our circumstances, there was always room for kindness, laughter, and the forging of lifelong friendships.

Our three-week stay in the camp, which we affectionately named "The Refugees' Haven," forever left an indelible mark on our hearts. It was a chapter in our lives filled with unexpected beauty, strength, and resilience. It became a testament to the power of human kindness and the unyielding spirit within each of us.

Though our time in The Refuge's Haven was temporary, the memories and lessons we gained will remain etched in our souls forever. It restored hope, provided laughter, and rekindled dreams. As we bid farewell to this oasis during our refugee journey, we carried with us the unwavering belief that no matter the challenges that lay ahead, we would face them with courage, unity, and the knowledge that even in the darkest of times, there is always a glimmer of light.

18

From a Camp to a Dream Home

It had been three weeks since our arrival at the camp. Little did we know our lives were about to take a momentous turn, transforming our existence into a blissful symphony of joy and prosperity.

With bated breath and hearts brimming with anticipation, we were summoned to the administrative office. As we entered, excitement permeated the air, electrifying our spirits. We were about to embark on a journey that would forever alter the trajectory of our lives.

In that momentous meeting, someone greeted us with the most extraordinary news—our days of residing within the confines of the camp were ending. We would be moving into a glorious oasis the next day: a low-cost apartment on Lage's outskirts. This dreamlike modest residence encompassed three exquisite bedrooms, each promising a sanctuary of comfort and tranquility.

The mere thought of stepping into our new home, adorned with the promises of a brighter future, sent delight down our spines. Our hearts danced in unison, embracing the joyous rhythm of this newfound opportunity. We envisioned a life filled with laughter, love, and limitless possibilities.

As we bid farewell to the camp, our souls were ablaze with gratitude, for destiny had showered us with an extraordinary stroke of fortune. The journey from the camp to our dream home was not merely a physical transition, but a profound metaphorical metamorphosis. It symbolized a rebirth and a renaissance of our spirits as we stepped into a world where dreams were no longer a distant mirage but a tangible reality within our grasp.

Our new apartment became our sanctuary, a place where dreams took flight. My father, a man of unyielding determination, embraced the life of a long-haul truck driver. Though he was often away during the week, his presence on weekends brought immeasurable joy to our humble dwelling. He would regale us with tales of his adventures on the open road, and we would listen, wide-eyed and captivated.

And my remarkable mother was the true magician of our household. Her remarkable taste and eye for beauty transformed our apartment into respite of warmth and love. The Salvation Army became her treasure trove, where she would spend hours hunting for hidden gems. Each piece she lovingly collected added a touch of elegance to our home, creating an ambiance that whispered of dreams fulfilled.

Our journey to freedom was a challenging one. When we made our daring escape from the clutches of East Germany, I was just a young lad of fourteen, and my education was abruptly halted. But life has a way of granting second chances, and destiny smiled upon me in the welcoming arms of Lage. I resumed my education, joining the sixth grade and embarking on a quest to conquer the knowledge I had missed.

The teachers and students of Lage embraced me with open hearts and minds, recognizing the determination burning within me. With unwavering support and guidance, I completed the remaining two years of grades seven and eight and soared to new heights of academic excellence. It was as if the challenges of the past had only fueled my thirst for knowledge, propelling me toward a future filled with infinite possibilities.

In the years that followed, our family continued to thrive, painting the canvas of our lives with vibrant hues of success and joy. I emerged as a beacon of inspiration, my educational journey symbolizing resilience and triumph over adversity.

The incredible strength and tenacity that saw us through our darkest moments humbles me as I look back on the tapestry of my life. Our story is a testament to the indomitable spirit of the human heart, a reminder that hope can guide us to calmer shores even in the harshest storms. It is a tale that uplifts and inspires, urging others to embrace their journeys and overcome the hurdles that stand in their way.

I celebrate our triumphs. I always remember that within each of us lies the power to transform adversity into opportunity and create a legacy that will shine brightly for generations to come.

19

Mastering the Art of Metal

In 1958, at age seventeen, I perceived the world to be filled with endless possibilities, and dreams appeared within arm's reach. During this pivotal moment, I completed my formal education. Little did I know that this would begin a remarkable adventure that would shape me into the person I am today.

Filled with ambition and brimming with curiosity, I embarked on a path that would forever change my destiny. The renowned machine shop Walter Brand in the enchanting town of Lage granted me the opportunity to begin my apprenticeship as a toolmaker. The mere thought of stepping into this esteemed establishment sent excitement down my spine.

As the days unfolded, I discovered this apprenticeship was no ordinary endeavor. It was a rigorous and demanding journey that required unwavering dedication and a hunger to learn. I carefully crafted my schedule each week, dedicating Mondays, Wednesdays, and Fridays to toiling away at the machine shop, while reserving Tuesdays and Thursdays for school. This unique arrangement allowed me to immerse myself in every facet of the business, gaining a comprehensive understanding of the art of metalworking.

The challenges I faced during this period were no small feat. They tested my limits, pushed me to exhaustion, and demanded perfection. But it was through these obstacles that I indeed discovered the extent of my capabilities. I immersed myself in the intricate world of metal, learning to mold it with my hands, shape it with precision, and breathe life into raw materials.

One defining moment that stands out vividly is the final examination that awaited me at the culmination of my apprenticeship. It was a trial like no other, a test of skill and craftsmanship that would determine whether I was worthy of bearing the title of primary toolmaker. The examination comprised a grueling written test and the formidable task of fashioning a functional lock from a raw piece of steel measuring 6" x 8" x 3". The catch? No power tools were to be used, and no shortcuts were to be taken. Every cut and every hone had to be executed by the sheer force of my hands.

The intensity of those three days was unparalleled. With beads of sweat cascading down my brow, I meticulously chiseled away at the steel, pouring every ounce of my being into crafting a masterpiece. Doubt occasionally whispered in my ear, tempting me to succumb to its grip, but my unwavering determination drowned out its voice. I refused to let anything hinder my progress, for I knew that within me lay the power to overcome any challenge that stood in my way.

When the time came to present my creation, a sense of pride and accomplishment filled my entire being. The lock stood before me, a testament to the countless hours of labor and the many moments of doubt that I had conquered. It shone with an ethereal brilliance, symbolizing resilience and unwavering dedication.

Admiration danced in his gaze as the examiner's eyes grazed over my work. He nodded approvingly, confirming what I had known: I had succeeded. At that moment, I realized the magnitude of my potential and the boundless horizons that awaited me in the world of craftsmanship.

From that day forward, the world seemed to open its arms to me, beckoning me to explore its vast wonders. The future shone bright with infinite possibilities, and I was eager to seize every one. That experience at Walter Brand not only transformed me into a master of my craft, it also instilled an unyielding belief in my abilities, that I could conquer any challenge. But this chapter at Walter Brand wasn't all about hard work and success; it's also the story of falling in love for the first time.

As I stood before the Walter Brand Company entrance gate daily, anticipation coursed through my veins. And there, like a vision from a dream, a young enchantress named Brigitte Klein emerged. She captivated my heart with her radiant smile, for it seemed like the sun had bestowed warmth upon her lips. Her beauty was unparalleled—tall, slender, with a grace in her stride that spoke of untold secrets and unspoken desires.

Unable to resist the magnetic pull of her charm, I summoned every ounce of courage and asked her for a date. To my delight, she accepted, and my heart danced with joy. In my excitement, I vowed to make this date an experience that would forever linger in her memory, for I was determined to sweep her off her feet and into a world of romance.

Determined, I broke open my piggy bank, releasing nearly forty German Marks. The sum may have seemed meager to some, but it represented a fortune, a testament to the lengths I would go to make this evening unforgettable. With my newfound wealth, I swiftly made a reservation at the illustrious Hotel League, a haven of luxury and refinement and a restaurant renowned for its culinary delights.

On that magical night, as I awaited Brigitte's arrival, my heart raced like a wild stallion, pounding against my chest with an intensity that matched the fiery passion that burned within me. And then, there she was, a vision in a delicate dress stressing her every curve. Her eyes sparkled with anticipation, mirroring my own, as we embarked upon an evening that would change our lives forever.

Within the walls of that charming hotel, time seemed to stand still as our souls intertwined and our hearts danced to the rhythm of love. We laughed, shared stories, and reveled in each other's presence, and our connection deepened with every passing moment. The atmosphere was alive with electric energy, as if the surrounding air vibrated with the force of our burgeoning affection.

As the night wore on, it was enchantment: stolen glances, tender touches, whispered promises, and shared dreams. At that moment, the world outside ceased to exist, and we were the sole inhabitants of a universe built upon the foundations of love. It is a tale of how a chance encounter at the gates of Walter Brand transformed into my first love story.

20

A Divine Encounter: Meeting God

Reflecting on those years, a particular moment remains etched in my memory. It was a time of growth, both in my chosen career path and in my spiritual journey. The year was 1959, and I had just started my apprenticeship as a toolmaker at Walter Brand. Little did I know that during this challenging and triumphant time, an encounter with God would transform my life.

As the leaves danced in a gentle breeze one crisp autumn morning, I was entrusted with a significant responsibility. My father handed me an envelope with cash, the funds needed to cover our utility bills and rent. It was a task I had performed countless times before, but fate had a different plan for me this time.

Lost in contemplation, I strolled through a nearby park, seeking solace in the beauty of nature. Perched upon a tree, I observed the ebb and flow of people walking by, their lives intertwining in intricate patterns. Little did I realize that in this tranquil sanctuary my fate was about to take an unexpected turn.

My heart sank as I arrived at the local bank, only to discover the dreadful truth: The envelope containing the precious funds had vanished without a trace. Panic seized me as I grappled with the unimaginable consequences that awaited me upon returning home. I knew all too well the disappointment and anger that would consume my father, for I had let him down. Drowning in fear and uncertainty, I embarked on the long journey back home, each step heavy with the weight of my mistake. Thoughts raced through my mind, painting vivid pictures of the retribution that awaited me. I could already envision my father's disappointment etched upon his face, his usually kind eyes transformed by disappointment.

But after I'd gotten home and was awaiting with despair my father's return, I heard a knock at the door . With trembling hands, I summoned the courage to open it, revealing a mysterious older man, his face adorned with a majestic beard that seemed to hold secrets of the universe.

As I stood before him, empathy instantly moved my heart. His hunger and thirst were evident, and I couldn't bear to turn him away. Ignoring the cautionary words of my father, I made a decision that would forever change my life. With a flicker of uncertainty, I invited him into our kitchen. Opening the fridge, I placed every morsel of food on the table, urging him to eat to his heart's content. The older man's tired eyes lit up with gratitude, and a warm smile graced his weathered face. All of my worries vanished at that precise moment, and profound fulfillment took their place.

As I watched him relish the meal, my heart swelled with indescribable happiness. It was as if the troubles that had burdened me, like the lost envelope containing my father's hard-earned money, had suddenly become inconsequential. The universe seemed to align, and the divine presence of God enveloped me, filling every crevice of my being with a sense of purpose and serenity. Time seemed to stand still as the older man finished his meal, his gentle smile never wavering. Silently, he rose from his seat, and I escorted him back to the street, feeling an inexplicable connection between our souls.

It was a moment that transcended the boundaries of human understanding, as if a celestial being in disguise had graced me with its presence. Returning to the kitchen, a sense of awe washed over me as I discovered the envelope that had gone missing, sitting precisely where the older man had eaten. In that very instant, I knew without a doubt that I had experienced a divine encounter. It was as if God Himself had orchestrated this meeting, using the older man as an instrument to test my compassion and reward my selflessness. Tears of gratitude streamed down my face as I realized the magnitude of the blessings unfolding before me. It was a gentle reminder that acts of kindness are never in vain, no matter how small. In that humble kitchen, among the leftovers and the remnants of a simple meal shared, I witnessed the beauty of humanity and the divine presence that lives within us.

From that day forward, my life changed. I sought opportunities to extend a helping hand and comfort those in need. The encounter had ignited a fire within me to serve others selflessly, knowing that in doing so, I was fulfilling my purpose and connecting with the divine spark that lives within us all.

I share this story of a chance encounter turned divine appointment, hoping it may inspire others to embrace the beauty of compassion and the transfor-mative power of a single act of kindness. For in the tapestry of life, these moments weave together to create a world filled with love, light, and the presence of God.

21

Depths of the Sea -The Call to Adventure

In 1961, at age 21, as fate would have it, my apprenticeship at Walter Brand ended just as I fell in love with Brigitte, the enchanting gatekeeper of the factory. It was a bittersweet moment, for while my heart ached, I knew it was time to embark on a new chapter of my life. I yearned for something more splendid, an opportunity to expand my horizons, save money, and explore the vast wonders of the world. And so, with Europe beckoning me, I made a fateful decision: to become a machinist in the German Kriegsmarine, the mighty Navy. With sheer determination burning in my soul, I applied to join the Kriegsmarine, eager to prove myself in the sea's crucible. To my delight and trepidation, they accepted me into their ranks. Little did I know that this decision would plunge me into an extraordinary adventure that would test my mettle and ignite the fire within me.

After enduring challenging training, I was honored with my initial assign-ment: an impressive ship that had previously sailed under the stars and stripes during World War II. The German Kriegsmarine had recommissioned it, and now I was an integral part of its crew, entrusted with the mighty engines that powered this magnificent landing ship, LSM 45. Venturing deep into the ship's bowels, I descended into the heart of the engine room, where a symphony of machinery awaited my command. The air was thick with the scent of oil and the rhythmic rumble of colossal engines. It was where shadows danced upon the walls, and the hum of power thrummed through my very core. Days turned into nights as I toiled tirelessly, ensuring the ship's engines roared with unyielding vigor. I became one with the relentless ship's heartbeat, a conductor in this mechanical symphony that propelled us forward.

The Frozen Frontier: A Tale of Ice and Adventure

On a crisp morning in the heart of winter, I learned about my unique three-month assignment. Six long months had passed since I last set foot on that old American landing ship LSM45, tirelessly serving as a machinist in the ship's belly. This opportunity, however, would be entirely different. I was to embark on an icebreaker under a civilian contract with the navy, tasked with keeping the treacherous North Atlantic shipping lane passable for the mighty German Navy Fleet.

The mere thought of not having to wear the uniform or adhere to the rigidity of naval discipline was a welcome respite. My shoulders felt lighter, and excitement flowed through my veins. I could hardly contain my excitement at the adventure ahead of me. As I boarded the icebreaker, the bitter winter winds whipped through the air, biting at my exposed skin and reminding me of the challenging conditions that awaited us.

The vessel itself was a marvel, a massive steel behemoth designed to conquer the icy depths of the unforgiving ocean. The crew members, a motley group of individuals from diverse backgrounds, greeted me with warmth and camaraderie, instantly making me feel at home. Our mission, while seemingly straightforward, was fraught with danger and uncertainty. Our task was to forge a path through the icy expanse, battling against nature's relentless grip. Every day, we would venture into uncharted territory, braving the elements in our quest to keep the shipping lane open.

Life on the icebreaker was unlike anything I had ever experienced. During the days, time seemed to stretch on forever, and the nights felt even longer. With only a faint touch, the sun greeted the horizon, spreading an otherworldly shimmer over the frozen scenery. The biting cold gnawed our bones, and the constant howling winds were a haunting reminder of our isolation from the rest of the world. The crew came together as a close-knit group, because we shared a common goal. We relied on each other's expertise and unwavering determination to overcome the challenges before us. In the engine rooms, the true heart of the icebreaker, I found solace in my familiar role as a machinist. The rhythmic hum of the engines provided both comfort and a sense of purpose, reminding me of the vital role we played in this frozen dance with destiny. Each passing day brought new obstacles, testing our mettle and pushing us to our limits.

We encountered towering icebergs that threatened to engulf our vessel, their majestic beauty concealing the danger that lurked beneath the surface. But we persevered, using our ice-breaking prowess to carve a path through the frozen wilderness. Despite the harsh conditions, we found moments of respite and wonder. The icebreaker, a testament to human ingenuity, became our trusted ally in this battle against nature's icy grip.

Finally, after what felt like an eternity, our three-month assignment ended. As we sailed back toward civilization, I couldn't help but reflect on this experience's profound impact. It was a chapter in my life that reminded me of the boundless possibilities beyond the confines of the familiar, beckoning us to embrace the unknown and embark on extraordinary journeys.

22

A New Beginning in the Shadows of Adversity

As my service in the German Kriegsmarine (Navy) neared its end in 1958, I sensed a profound change within my family. The once-vibrant love between my parents had withered, leaving behind a bitter residue of resentment. This transformation pained me deeply, but duty called, and I embarked on my final naval journey, unaware of the long-simmering tensions at home.

The roots of our family's turmoil stretched back to World War II, where my father had witnessed unspeakable atrocities. These experiences left an indelible mark on his soul, manifesting in haunting flashbacks and relentless nightmares. A heavy cloud of depression hung over our home, its impact amplified by the era's lack of understanding of and treatment for mental health issues.

The Aftermath of Divorce

In the wake of my parents' divorce, I noticed a shift in my father's demeanor toward me. His affection seemed to dwindle, and I felt he viewed me as a disappointment. This was deeply disheartening, but I later came to understand that his behavior stemmed from his own internal struggles rather than a lack of love.

My father, once a brave soldier, now grappled with the psychological aftermath of war. It was as if the conflict had taken a piece of him, leaving him adrift in the complexities of postwar life. In his search for solace and a fresh start, he remarried shortly after the divorce. At the time, this seemed sudden to me, but I now recognize it as his attempt to find happiness and stability.

A Life Cut Short

Tragically, my father's life was cut short at the age of 71. Receiving the news of his passing was bittersweet; while grief enveloped me, I chose to focus on the positive moments we had shared and the invaluable lessons he had imparted.

Through my father's tough love, I learned resilience and determination. His belief in my abilities, even when he struggled to express it, motivated me to prove myself. Every achievement, big or small, became a testament to those rare times he encouraged me.

Reflections on Our Relationship

Looking back, I realize that my father's aloofness was his way of coping with our family's immense changes. The divorce had shaken the foundation of our lives, and he, like many others, grappled with finding his place in this new reality. His behavior was not a reflection of his love for me but rather a manifestation of his internal battles.

So, as I reminisce about my father, I choose to remember the tender moments we shared—him teaching me to ride a bike, the laughter we shared during family vacations, and the unspoken support that pushed me to be the best version of myself. His struggles do not define him entirely. They serve as a reminder of his resilience and strength. My father's legacy lives on within me, inspiring me to face life's challenges head-on and cherish the love we once had.

Brotherly Bonds

Amid these family dynamics, my relationship with my brother Peter remained a constant source of comfort. We were inseparable companions in childhood, creating countless cherished memories. As we ventured into adulthood, our paths led us both to serve in the navy at age 18. Though we sailed on separate ships and seldom met during our time in service, the bond of brotherhood remained unbreakable, a testament to the enduring power of family ties.

Upon completing his naval tenure, Peter embarked on a new chapter in the merchant marine for the next six years, charting his course across the vast oceans. Meanwhile, I steadfastly pursued my career in Germany, fueled by a passion for adventure and service to our nation. Our shared experiences in the military instilled in us a sense of duty and camaraderie that would shape our lives forever.

At 28, Peter's heart was forever changed when he met the enchanting Barbel in the picturesque city of Hamburg, Germany. Their love story was one for the ages, filled with laughter, joy, and two precious gifts: their children, Andrea and Thorsten. Together, they navigated life's ups and downs, always standing strong by each other's side.

But tragedy struck in 2012, and Peter's world was shattered. His beloved Barbel was taken from him too soon, leaving a void in his heart that seemed impossible to fill. The pain of her loss weighed heavily on his soul, casting a shadow over his once-vibrant spirit. Peter found himself lost in a sea of grief, struggling to find a way to carry on without the love of his life by his side.

Yet, through the darkness, a glimmer of hope began to emerge. Peter realized that Barbel's love had not disappeared with her passing; it lived on in the memories they had created together, their children's laughter, and the strength he found to keep going. With each passing day, Peter's heart healed a little more, and he began to see that love never truly dies, it simply transforms into something new, something beautiful, something that would guide him toward a brighter tomorrow.

As Peter entered his late seventies, the cruel grip of dementia began to tighten its hold on his mind. Yet, a beacon of light emerged in the form of his devoted daughter, Andrea. With unwavering love and compassion, she became his rock, caregiver, and lifeline in a sea of confusion and forgetfulness.

Peter's memory slipped further and further away in 2023, marking a poignant chapter in his life. Each visit became a bittersweet dance of fleeting recognition and heartbreaking confusion. But in those precious moments of clarity, when his eyes sparkled with flickers of memory, it was as if the Peter we knew and loved was still there, fighting valiantly against the encroaching shadows of his illness.

Though the pain of witnessing his decline was a heavy burden to bear, the memories we shared during those visits became treasures to hold onto. We laughed, we cried, and we reminisced about the adventures of our youth, weaving a tapestry of love and nostalgia that would remain etched in our hearts forever. Peter's unwavering strength and resilience in the face of such adversity were a powerful reminder of the indomitable human spirit, a beacon of hope and inspiration to all who knew him.

A Mother's Strength

My mother, a pillar of strength, bore the brunt of my father's inner turmoil. Day after day, she soldiered on, trying to rekindle the fading flame of their love. But alas, even the strongest hearts can break, and one fateful day, my mother made the heart-wrenching decision to leave our family home behind.

With a heavy heart and unshed tears, she sought solace in Bielefeld, Westfalia, a city twenty-six miles away from our residence in Lage/Lippe.

The journey toward Bielefeld was not just a physical one for my mother, but a journey of resilience and hope against all odds. With little more than her shattered dreams and raw determination, she faced the harsh reality of poverty. In those days, the courts often favored the husband, leaving women like my mother vulnerable to financial insecurity. Yet, she found strength in her vulnerability through the darkest nights. She rebuilt her life brick by brick, refusing to let the weight of despair crush her spirit. Every setback was met with unwavering resolve, and every obstacle was transformed into an opportunity for growth.

She learned to navigate the labyrinthine legal system, fighting tooth and nail for her rights and the rights of countless other women who found themselves in similar predicaments. But it wasn't just the external battles that defined her journey. Within the confines of her new life, she faced an internal struggle, grappling with the unfamiliarity of starting over. The bustling avenues of Bielefeld replaced the once-familiar streets of Lage/Lippe. Every corner held a new story, every face an unknown chapter waiting to be explored. It was daunting, but my mother refused to let fear consume her. With unwavering determination, my mother sought employment, even in the face of limited opportunities. She toiled day and night, embracing every menial job that came her way. The work was grueling and the pay was meager, but she found solace in the fact that she was forging her own path, reclaiming her independence, and providing for herself.

As time passed, the wounds gradually healed, and my mother began to rebuild her life from the ground up. She found solace in the friendships she forged, the community that embraced her, and the newfound freedom she had rediscovered. Her struggles were not easily forgotten but became stepping stones on her journey toward self-discovery.

Looking back, it is impossible to fully comprehend the immense strength it took for my mother to endure such hardships. The weight of uncertainty, financial instability, and emotional turmoil must have been overwhelming. Yet, through it all, she never lost sight of the light at the end of the tunnel. Through my mother's unwavering strength, I have learned that even in despair, hope can flicker like a candle flame, guiding us toward a brighter tomorrow.

My Post-Navy Years

When I returned from the Navy at age 21, I boldly decided to move to Bielefeld, Westfalia, and live with my mother. She had a cozy two-bedroom apartment, with one room for my sister and another for my brother and me. While my brother was mainly away serving in the navy and then the merchant marine, my mother found a fantastic job at Gundlach, a prestigious printing company.

I had a burning desire to further my education, so I enrolled in a computer science program. Over the next two years, I immersed myself in coding and programming, sharpening my skills and expanding my knowledge. It was a challenging journey that I embraced with enthusiasm and determination. After completing my studies, I set my sights on finding employment that would allow me to apply my newfound expertise. That's when I landed a job at Stork, a renowned chocolate-manufacturing company famous for their delectable Merci Chocolate boxes. I joined their team as a computer operator and programmer, ready to take on any technological challenge that came my way.

I became engrossed in the fascinating world of computers on my first day. The intricacies of programming and operating systems enthralled me, and I thrived in this environment. The constant innovation and problem-solving required in my role pushed me to excel and surpass expectations. My career choice of computer science has been one of the best decisions I've ever made. It has opened doors to opportunities and allowed me to pursue my passion with unwavering dedication. As I continued to grow and evolve in this field, I was grateful for the boldness that led me down this path and was excited for the incredible future. But working for a great company like Stork had other side benefits.

Sweet Memories of Stork Chocolate: A Taste of Heaven

Every morning as I approached the factory, a delightful aroma of sweet chocolate enveloped me. Stork was known for its commitment to using only the freshest ingredients in crafting their delectable chocolates. And I can still recall the sight of a magnificent stainless-steel truck, brimming with cooled-down sweet cream, rolling through the factory gates each day. This main ingredient would transform into the mouthwatering chocolate we knew and loved.

The towering stainless-steel drums stood proudly inside the factory, housing the secret blend of ingredients that would soon become the stuff of dreams. Among these ingredients was the sweet, precious cream, which added velvety richness to the chocolate. It was a sight to behold these drums reaching toward the heavens, filled with the promise of something truly extraordinary. But it wasn't just the visual spectacle that captivated us. The chemist, a master of his craft, was responsible for ensuring that each batch of chocolate met the highest standards of perfection. Throughout the process, he would carefully extract tiny samples from a spigot, testing and tasting them to ensure the chocolate was on par with Stork's impeccable reputation.

Now, let me share a little secret with you. Lunchtime at Stork was a memorable affair, and we chocolate enthusiasts had a little trick up our sleeves. We would eagerly gather around the stainless-steel drums, cup in hand, waiting for that perfect moment. When the time was right, we would position our cups beneath the spigot, eagerly anticipating that first taste of the warm, velvety mixture. Joy filled our hearts as we savored that moment! The rich, creamy chocolate would dance on our taste buds, leaving us with a sense of pure bliss. It was a secret indulgence, a stolen moment of pure chocolate heaven that we cherished.

As the years have passed, that time at Stork remains etched in my memory. The tantalizing aroma, the towering drums, and the clandestine lunchtime tastings all contributed to an experience that shaped my love for chocolate. It was a time of youthful enthusiasm, when the world of chocolate opened before me, revealing its secrets and captivating my senses. So, as I reflect on those sweet memories of Stork Chocolate, I am reminded of the passion and dedication that went into creating something truly extraordinary. Those days instilled in me a deep appreciation for the artistry and craftsmanship that go into creating such a delectable treat. It was a chapter in my life that I will always hold dear. I witnessed firsthand the magic that happens when fresh ingredients and a touch of creativity come together.

Enduring Friendships: The Sweet Bonds of Stork

During my time at Stork, I had the pleasure of forging friendships that have stood the test of time, lasting more than years. One such friend was Hartmut, affectionately known as Keule, who had a knack for making me laugh. Not only was he a great companion, but he also had a way with the ladies. We would often benefit from his popularity, as hanging out with Keule meant we could meet new girls and create unforgettable memories.

Another remarkable friend I made at Stork was Jochen. Jochen had an incredible intellect and a talent for fixing almost anything. His parents owned a farmhouse that they had converted into a charming restaurant. Little did I know that this farmhouse held a hidden gem in its attic: a party room known as the "party *boden.*" Through Jochen, I had the privilege of discovering this secret haven. During one of our visits to the party boden, I had the pleasure of meeting Jochen's beautiful sister, Jutta. From the moment our eyes met, I was secretly smitten, though I never found the courage to admit my feelings to her. Despite this unspoken love, Jutta and I remained the best of friends throughout our lives, sharing countless adventures and treasured moments.

The bonds formed during those Stork days were exceptional. We laughed together, supported one another, and created memories that would last a lifetime. The camaraderie we shared extended far beyond the walls of the chocolate factory, weaving its way into the fabric of our lives. As the years passed, our friendships only grew stronger. We celebrated milestones, weathered storms, and embraced life's joys and challenges. Through it all, the foundation of our friendship remained steadfast, built upon a shared history and a deep understanding of one another. Looking back, I am grateful for the friendships that blossomed at Stork. These connections enriched my life in ways I could never have imagined. They taught me the value of laughter, the importance of loyalty, and the power of enduring bonds.

So, as I reflect on those cherished friendships, I am reminded of their profound impact on my life. The laughter shared with Keule, the ingenuity of Jochen, and the unspoken love for Jutta—all these experiences have shaped me into the person I am today. They taught me the importance of embracing joy, finding humor in life's ups and downs, and cherishing the bonds we form with others. These friendships have been a constant source of support, love, and companionship, guiding me through the various chapters of my life. We have celebrated birthdays, weddings, and children's births together. We have stood by each other's side during loss and heartache, offering a shoulder to lean on and a listening ear. Our friendship has weathered the tests of time, proving that authentic connections can withstand any obstacle.

So, as I continue my journey, I carry the lessons learned from these enduring friendships. They have taught me the value of loyalty, the beauty of shared experiences, and the importance of being there for one another. I am forever grateful for the friendships that blossomed during my time at Stork, as they have enriched my life in immeasurable ways. And so, I raise a toast to Keule, Jochen, Jutta, and all the friends who have walked alongside me for years. Thank you for the laughter, the love, and the unwavering support. Cheers to enduring friendships, the sweetest gift life has to offer.

23

The Summer of 1970: A Journey to America Begins, a Dream Takes Flight

I vividly remember the summer of 1970 as if it were just yesterday. It was a time of excitement and anticipation, and little did I know it would mark the beginning of a remarkable journey for my sister, Karla.

It was a typical day when I returned home from work, tired and ready to unwind. Karla, my then-32-year-old big sister, welcomed me with joy shining on her face. She waved a piece of paper in her hand, twirling around and singing a merry tune.

"I am going to America!" she exclaimed, her voice filled with pure delight. For the past six months, Karla has been tirelessly working on obtaining a visitor's visa to the United States. It had been a long and arduous process, filled with paperwork, interviews, and countless waiting periods. But finally, she had received the long-awaited green light from the American consulate. Her dream of setting foot on American soil was about to become a reality.

Unlike my sister, I had been fortunate enough to explore various European countries. Karla had never ventured beyond the borders of our homeland. This trip to America would be her first taste and endless possibilities of the world beyond. We had distant relatives, Uncle Werner and Aunt Edna, who lived in the vibrant city of Philadelphia. They stayed in touch through letters and visits. Unfortunately, when they visited, I was away serving in the Navy and never met them.

Karla's departure date was August 10, and she would embark on a multi-stop journey. From Frankfurt, she would fly to the enchanting land of Reykjavik, Iceland, before continuing her voyage to the bustling City of New York. Finally, her destination would be the northeast section of Philadelphia. As we bid farewell to Karla on that bittersweet day, our emotions were a mix of sadness and joy. We were sad to see her go, knowing we would miss her dearly during her time away.

When Karla stepped off the plane in New York, her heart raced with anticipation. As she entered the bustling airport, she spotted Uncle Werner and Aunt Edna waiting at the customs exit. Their long-lost relative Karla had finally reunited with them on American soil, and their faces lit up with joy as they embraced. Karla couldn't help but tremble with excitement as a mixture of anxiety and happiness overcame her.

Communication posed a challenge in those early days. Karla's command of the English language was limited, and Uncle Werner and Aunt Edna could only speak a smattering of German. But their shared love and familial bond bridged the language barrier, and they understood each other. It was a time of patience and learning as they navigated through conversations with gestures, simple phrases, and the occasional translation dictionary.

The first few months in America proved to be challenging for Karla. Everything was unfamiliar, from the language to the customs and way of life. Determined to make the most of her time in America, Uncle Werner and Aunt Edna wasted no time enrolling Karla in English classes five days a week. They knew mastering the language would be crucial for her success and integration into American society.

Karla's dedication and hard work paid off. After six months of intensive language study, she became proficient in English and felt more confident navigating her new surroundings. With her newfound language skills, she took the next step and applied for a job at Provident National Bank, now known as PNC Bank. It was a significant milestone for Karla as she embarked on her professional journey in America.

Like many Americans, Aunt Edna was obsessed with hair styling and hairspray. In Germany, Karla had never encountered such emphasis on perfectly styled hair. Much to Karla's bewilderment, Aunt Edna insisted on restyling her hair and ensuring it stayed in place with hairspray. It was a cultural difference that took some getting used to, but Karla embraced it as part of her American experience.

Another challenge arose with language usage. Aunt Edna was adamant that Karla only speak English during family gatherings. She would become visibly upset if Karla conversed in German with guests who knew the language. It was a source of tension and frustration for Karla during her first year in America. She longed to connect with her German roots and converse freely in her native language. The restriction on speaking German at family gatherings made her feel isolated and disconnected from her cultural heritage. Karla yearned for comfort in her mother's presence, believing that having her by her side would ease some of her challenges.

As time passed, Karla's resilience and determination paid off. She found solace in the friendships she formed with fellow English class students, who were also navigating the complexities of adapting to a new country. Together, they shared their experiences, supported one another, and formed a tight-knit community that helped ease the homesickness and loneliness. Karla's relationship with Aunt Edna gradually strengthened as well. While there were still moments of disagreement and cultural clashes, they found common ground and a deeper understanding of each other's perspectives. Aunt Edna realized that Karla's German heritage was integral to her identity, and she started to embrace and appreciate the richness of their shared cultural background.

As the months turned into years, Karla's love for America grew. She witnessed the country's vibrant diversity, boundless opportunities, and the spirit of resilience permeating every aspect of American life. Karla's journey to America had transformed her in ways she had never imagined. She had become a stronger, more independent woman, capable of navigating the challenges of a new country and embracing the beauty of its differences. And so, as the summer of 1970 unfolded, Karla's story continued. The next chapter of her American adventure awaited, filled with new experiences, triumphs, and the possibility of reuniting with her beloved mother. The journey had just begun, and Karla was ready to embrace every twist and turn ahead.

24

Across the Ocean: A Tale of Love and Sacrifice

I recall my mother's unwavering dedication to maintaining a heartfelt connection with my beloved sister, Karla. She poured her soul onto delicate airmail paper each week, eagerly expecting a response. Remarkably, even before receiving a reply, she would already have the following letter prepared, ready to embark on its transatlantic journey. The distinct markings on that particular paper, denoting its purpose for airmail, remain etched in my mind. In those days, sending mail through the air was a luxury reserved for the privileged few. It was an expense that not everyone could afford. Oh, how times have changed! Nowadays, a quick phone call to America is a trivial matter, but it was a privilege reserved for the wealthy back then. Even if one could make a call, the operator only allowed a brief conversation. Can you fathom the notion? The mere thought of conversing with someone across the ocean, even for a few precious minutes, was an almost unimaginable feat.

The temptation to sneak a peek at my mother's heartfelt letters before they embarked on their transoceanic journey was irresistible. I yearned to understand the depth of her longing for my sister, Karla. The words etched on those pages resonated with a profound sense of yearning and love, desperately seeking to bridge the physical chasm that separated them. My mother's heart yearned for the day she could reunite with her beloved daughter, leaving behind her life in Germany to embark on a fresh start in America. When my mother sought my opinion, I did not hesitate. I wholeheartedly encouraged her, ensuring I would visit her every year during my vacation. I understood the magnitude of her desire and I was determined to support her in any way possible.

In the spring of 1973, with unwavering determination and unyielding courage, my mother embarked on a transformative journey that would forever alter the course of our lives. As I reflect upon those heartfelt letters and the sacrifices she made, I cannot help but admire her indomitable spirit. Propelled by her love for Karla, she crossed the vast ocean and forged a bond that will forever be etched in our hearts.

25

A Journey of Love and Adventure: From Oldendorf to America

As my mother settled into her new life in America and reunited with her beloved daughter Karla, I was at a crossroads. It was time for a change, a new chapter in my life. With a heavy heart, I cleared out my mother's apartment, bidding farewell to the place that held so many memories. It was time to move to Oldendorf Kreis Halle, a charming district in Halle Westfalen, to be closer to the Stork Chocolate Company, where I had worked for several years. No longer would I have to endure long train rides to work; I could now hop on my bike and enjoy a leisurely commute.

Over the next two years, I divided my time between my new life in Oldendorf and visiting my mother and sister in America. The distance between us no longer seemed impossible, and the joy of reuniting with my family was immeasurable. However, as each visit ended, I couldn't help but feel a longing to stay longer and to immerse myself in America's vibrant culture and breathtaking landscapes. With this desire burning within me, I made a bold decision.

Just before planning my third visit, I applied to the American consulate for a temporary visa, hoping to extend my stay in America. Three months later, I received the news I eagerly awaited: My visa was approved. It was a moment of pure joy, tinged with a hint of sadness, as I prepared to say goodbye to my job and bid farewell to my friends. But before I embarked on this grand adventure, I knew I had to celebrate this new chapter in my life. And what better way to bid farewell to my old life than with a spectacular going-away party?

It was a night filled with laughter, music, and heartfelt goodbyes. The memories of that evening were hazy, as the festivities carried on well into the night. I arrived at the airport with a slight hangover, full of excitement and anticipation for the trip ahead. And so, my multi-stop voyage began. From Frankfurt, I boarded a plane for Reykjavik. The rugged beauty of the Icelandic landscape left me in awe as I marveled at the majestic waterfalls and otherworldly geothermal wonders. It was a brief stopover that left an indelible mark on my soul. I continued my voyage from Reykjavik to New York. As soon as I arrived, I fell completely in love with the Big Apple's vibrant energy and well-known landmarks. The towering skyscrapers, the bustling streets, and the diverse array of cultures that coexisted harmoniously—it was a city unlike any other. I spent my days exploring Central Park, wandering through the bustling streets of Times Square, and immersing myself in this incredible metropolis's rich history and culture.

But my journey didn't end there. Philadelphia beckoned, and I eagerly looked forward to reuniting with my mother and sister there. As I stepped off the train at 30th Street Station, my heart raced with anticipation. It had been too long since I had seen their faces, heard their laughter, and felt their warm embrace. The moment I looked at them, it was as if time stood still. We embraced, tears of joy streaming down our faces, and I knew then that all the sacrifices and challenges I had faced were worth it.

In the following years, I established a new life in America with my family's love and support. I found a job that fulfilled me, made new friends who became like family, and embraced this new land's opportunities. But no matter how much time passed, the memories of that journey from Oldendorf to America remained etched in my heart.

I am filled with gratitude for the experiences, the challenges, and the love that guided me through this journey. It was one that shaped me into the person I am today, who understands the value of love, sacrifice, and pursuing happiness.

26

A Journey of Heritage and Hospitality at the German Society of Pennsylvania

When I first arrived in America, excitement and anticipation filled my heart. Little did I know my journey would lead me to the German Society of Pennsylvania. This place would become a home for my family and a hub of cultural exchange and celebration. Located on the historic 611 Springarden Street, the Society's building stood tall, emanating a sense of pride and tradition. It was a structure that seemed to hold within its walls the stories of countless immigrants who had come before me, seeking a better life in this land of opportunity.

My mother and sister, who had already made a name for themselves in the German Society, welcomed me with open arms. They lived in a spacious apartment connected to the main building through a three-story structure on Marshal Street. It was a place where the past intertwined with the present, bridging the gap between generations.

A woman of remarkable talent and dedication, my mother held the esteemed position of business agent at the German Society. Even with the impressive-sounding title, her responsibilities were much more extensive than they seemed at first glance. She was the driving force behind every event, meticulously planning and executing affairs that brought the community together.

From the Hamburger Abend to the New Year's party, from concerts to fundraising dinners, my mother's touch was evident in every detail. Her culinary skills were legendary, and her ability to entertain and host with grace and charm was unmatched. Members of the German Society held her in high regard, recognizing her as the heart and soul of their gatherings. But her role extended far beyond event planning. She was a trustworthy caretaker, ensuring that every space within the German Society was immaculate and restored to its former glory after each occasion. Her dedication knew no bounds, and her commitment to preserving the traditions of our German heritage was unwavering.

As I settled into my new life during those early days, I immersed myself in the vibrant atmosphere of the German Society. I worked tirelessly with my mother and sister, lending a hand wherever needed. As I helped organize events and connect with fellow members, I also embarked on a journey to master the English language, knowing that it would open doors to employment opportunities. The German Society of Pennsylvania became more than just a place of residence for me; it became a sanctuary of cultural exchange, a testament to the strength and resilience of the German American community. People upheld traditions, shared stories, and forged friendships in this place.

As time passed, I witnessed the Society develop and adapt to the changing times, and it became a place where diversity was celebrated and embraced. New generations of immigrants brought their own unique experiences and perspectives. Over the years, the German Society continued to thrive, hosting many events that showcased the richness of German culture. Something was always happening within its walls, from traditional dances to art exhibitions, language classes, and historical lectures. It became a beacon of heritage and hospitality, where people from all walks of life could come together and feel a sense of belonging.

Reflecting on my time there, I am grateful for the opportunities it provided me and my family. Within those walls, I learned the English language and discovered the power of community and the importance of preserving our cultural roots. Today, the German Society of Pennsylvania stands as a testament to the enduring spirit of the German-American community. People still honor traditions, forge friendships, and preserve the legacy of our ancestors at the German Society of Pennsylvania. In conclusion, my time there was filled with growth, connection, and a deep appreciation for the power of heritage.

27

From Limited English to Limitless Opportunities

Although my English was still limited, I burned with determination to find a job in the field of technology. Eager to overcome the language barrier, I asked my sister Karla to accompany me to an employment agency as my interpreter. Her English had flourished during our time in America, and she graciously agreed to help. Little did we know that this decision would lead to a life-changing opportunity.

The interview at the employment agency went remarkably well. Filled with hope and excitement, we returned home, only to have the phone ring moments later. The agency informed me they had selected me for an interview at AAA, the prestigious American Automobile Club. The IT manager requested I bring Karla along, as he was aware of my limited English and believed her presence would facilitate a more comprehensive conversation about my knowledge and background.

Filled with anticipation, we arrived at the interview, ready to showcase my skills and passion for technology. The conversation flowed effortlessly; I even offered to work without pay until they felt comfortable with me. To my surprise, the IT manager chuckled and explained that paying employees from the start in America was customary.

We shook hands, and he assured me he would contact me if they were interested in hiring me. As we exited the building, my sister shared advice she had learned along the way. "If anyone says, 'Don't call us, we'll call you,' it means you didn't get the job," she said. We returned home, hoping for the best but preparing for the possibility of disappointment. To our astonishment, AAA had left a message for us as soon as we walked through the door, offering me the job and instructing me to report to work the following Monday.

But the offer came with a unique condition: They asked me to bring Karla to assist with questions or translations that might arise during my early days at the company. Overwhelmed with joy, I couldn't contain my excitement. This was the breakthrough I had been waiting for, and I was eager to prove myself in the world of technology. Karla was excited, too. For the next few months, she became my trusted companion and guide, helping me navigate the intricacies of my new workplace. On that fateful Monday morning, we arrived at AAA, ready to embark on this exciting journey together. As we entered the office, I couldn't help but feel a mix of nerves and anticipation. The IT manager greeted us warmly, appreciating my sister's support in bridging language gaps.

Unveiling the Enigmatic World of 1970s Computer Marvels

In the AAA computer department, three sections held the power to shape the future: data entry, the tabulations room, and the awe-inspiring computer room.

Now, picture this: as I stepped into the tabulations room, a symphony of IBM equipment serenaded me. It was like entering a utopia of technological wonders. Back then, computers relied on a peculiar method called punch-card input and output. Imagine cards, not much bigger than your palm, carrying the essential information that governs these magnificent machines.

In this room of endless possibilities, I encountered the card-sorting machines, card-merging machines, and the mighty card-tabulating machines. These colossal contraptions were the epitome of innovation. But what truly fascinated me were the removable panels, mesmerizing holes, and yards of wire that adorned these beasts, waiting to be moved and rearranged like a symphony conductor directing an orchestra.

The card-sorting machine was straightforward and easily tamed with a few programming maneuvers. However, the card-merging machine was a different story altogether. Its complexity teased my intellect, demanding a more intricate dance of wires and holes to unlock its true potential. But the true marvel was the tabulating machine—how it captivated my imagination! It was a majestic contraption, capable of handling the most elaborate programs. To bring it to life, one had to attach several hundred wires, each intricately woven into a tapestry of complexity. Oh, the thrill of connecting these wires, like a maestro crafting a symphony of commands! In this era of boundless exploration, those punch cards held the key to unlocking the universe's secrets. They were the conduits that connected us to this realm of infinite possibilities.

Reflecting on my time in the AAA computer department a half-century ago, my sister's presence proved invaluable. She effortlessly translated conversations, ensuring I understood instructions and could effectively communicate my ideas. Her unwavering support and dedication made my new role smoother than I could have imagined. As time passed, my English skills gradually improved, and I became more confident in expressing myself. My sister's role as my interpreter slowly diminished as I navigated the language barrier independently. It was a bittersweet moment, as I realized I had grown personally and professionally thanks to her unwavering support.

Looking back, I am grateful for the opportunity. It was not just a job, but a stepping stone toward a brighter future at AAA. The experience taught me the importance of perseverance, adaptability, and the power of having a solid support system.

In the years that followed, I continued to thrive in the technology field at AAA, taking on new challenges and embracing every opportunity that came my way.

28

A Chance Encounter at the Union League: Love, Laughter, and Eyeglasses

I remember the day like it was yesterday. The phone rang, and it was my dear mother, inviting me to join her at a black-tie affair at none other than the prestigious Union League in Philadelphia. Now, let me tell you, this was no ordinary event. It was the anniversary ball of the Plays & Players Theater, and my mother had received a special invitation. How could I resist such an opportunity?

Excitedly, I handpicked a dashing black tuxedo while my mother wore a stunning long evening gown. We were ready to make a grand entrance. As we entered the Union League, I couldn't help but feel a sense of awe. The grandeur of the place was breathtaking.

As we made our way to our prearranged seats, my eyes couldn't help but wander around the room. And that's when I saw her. A beautiful, slim, red-headed woman walked through the door with an air of elegance. To my surprise, she made a beeline for our table and took the empty seat beside me, accompanied by her male escort. Little did I know she was an actor performing at the Plays & Players Theater. Throughout the evening, I managed to steal a few moments to engage in delightful conversations with the enchanting

Betsy. And, oh, the dance we shared! I felt frozen, as if the world around me had ceased to exist.

But as the night drew to a close, she gave me the cold shoulder, disappearing into the night. I thought I had lost her forever. But fate had other plans. A month later, as I strolled through Center City, I came upon an eyeglass store. And there she was, working behind the counter! It took every ounce of courage to walk in and strike up a conversation. To my delight, she recognized me immediately, and that meant I must have made quite an impression on that fateful evening at the Union League. We agreed to have lunch the following day, and my heart soared joyfully.

From Hollywood Dream to Local Stardom: Betsy's Journey

As we sat down for our first date, Betsy shared a fascinating story that would forever change how I saw her. She began by telling me about her recent return from Hollywood, where she had been pursuing her dreams of becoming an actor. Betsy had appeared in several movies, one of which I distinctly remember her mentioning was "Where Angels Go Trouble Follows," a 1969 American comedy film.

The movie revolved around a group of mischievous Catholic schoolgirls, and Betsy played a memorable role in it. But what struck me the most was the honesty with which she spoke about her experiences in Hollywood. Betsy revealed it was a cutthroat industry, where getting a leading role often meant compromising one's integrity. She explained that decision-making individuals expected many to engage in sexual relationships to secure desirable roles. However, Betsy had a solid moral compass and refused to compromise herself in such a way. With a heavy heart, she left Hollywood behind and returned to her roots in Philadelphia.

But Betsy's passion for acting remained unwavering, and she sought solace in the local theater scene. At the Plays & Players Theater in Philadelphia, she found a new home for her talent and a community that appreciated her unwavering integrity. Betsy faced challenges and triumphs while pursuing her acting career in the local theater scene. She poured her heart and soul into every performance, captivating audiences with her raw talent and unwavering dedication. Her performances were a testament to her love for the craft and refusal to compromise her principles. As Betsy shared her story with me, I couldn't help but feel a deep admiration for her strength and resilience. She had chosen the path less traveled, forsaking the glitz and glamour of Hollywood for the authenticity and artistic fulfillment that the local theater scene provided.

29

Love Blossoms and Dreams Take Flight

After that magical first date, Betsy and I fell deeper and deeper in love with each passing day. Our hearts danced to the rhythm of our shared dreams, and it wasn't long before we took the next step on our journey together. We were ready to embark on a new adventure, hand in hand, as we moved in together. The shell of a home I had purchased near the enchanting Italian market in Philadelphia awaited our touch. It was a canvas of possibilities, a place where our love would weave its own story. Although the house was only partially renovated, we transformed the first floor into a testament to our passion and dedication. We created a space that would be our sanctuary. **B**etsy tackled the renovation process with her unwavering spirit and strong work ethi**c.** She was a force to be reckoned with, unafraid to get her hands dirty while transforming our house into a home. We painted walls, laid down flooring, built a fireplace, put in new windows, and filled every nook and cranny with our hopes and dreams.

As we settled into this quaint new home, our hearts whispered of a future filled with love, laughter, and the pitter-patter of little feet. We both longed to start a family and set our sights on making that dream a reality within a year. The anticipation of what lay ahead filled our days with excitement and joy.

While planning our future, my mother, residing in the esteemed German Society of Pennsylvania, offered us a gift beyond measure. She graciously extended her hand and offered to host our wedding in the Society's grand ballroom. Exchanging vows in such a magnificent setting filled our hearts with awe and gratitude.

My mother, a master of organization and culinary genius, took charge of every aspect of the wedding. She meticulously crafted a menu that would tantalize our guests' taste buds and took on the task of cooking everything herself. With the help of friends and family, the kitchen in the German Society became a hub of love and laughter as they prepared a feast fit for royalty.

When our wedding day finally arrived, it was a sight to behold. The grand ballroom of the German Society was transformed into a fairy tale setting, with twinkling lights and fragrant flowers adorning every corner. The old library, nestled in the heart of the Society, became a haven of warmth and celebration as our loved ones gathered to toast our love. The ceremony was a tapestry of emotions as we exchanged heartfelt vows and promised to love and cherish each other for all eternity. Our words were not just mere promises but a testament to the depth of our love and commitment to one another.

After the ceremony, the celebration continued in the enchanting library above the ballroom. The room was adorned with vintage books and delicate lace, creating an ambiance of timeless elegance. The air was filled with laughter, joy, and the clinking of glasses as our loved ones raised a toast to our happiness. The feast that awaited us was nothing short of a culinary masterpiece. The aroma of delectable dishes filled the air, enticing our senses and whetting our appetites. Each bite was a symphony of flavors, a testament to my mother's culinary prowess and the love she poured into every dish. As the night wore on, the dance floor became a stage for our passion to shine. We swayed to the music, lost in each other's arms as if the world around us ceased to exist. The room was filled with laughter and the sound of our loved ones celebrating our union, creating a symphony of joy that echoed in our hearts.

Looking back on that magical day, I am grateful for the love and support surrounding us. Our wedding was not just a celebration of our love but a testament to the power of family, friendship, and the bonds that hold us together.

30

A Love Reborn: Sabine's Arrival

We shared a dream to bring a child into our loving home after marriage. One fateful day, our dreams began to take shape with the joyous news that Betsy was carrying a precious life within her. Excitement filled our hearts as we realized we had only nine months to complete our home and create a beautiful nursery for our little one.

As we embarked on this journey, our love for each other grew stronger every day. We worked tirelessly, hand in hand, painting walls, hanging curtains, and filling the air with joyous anticipation. Our love was the foundation upon which our dreams were built, shining through every corner of our home.

During this time, we discovered we were blessed with a baby girl. Overwhelmed with joy, we embarked on a quest to find the perfect name for our little angel. With her gentle smile and twinkling eyes, Betsy suggested we honor my youngest sister, Sabine, who had left this world too soon. Sabine, born in November 1942, had tragically succumbed to diphtheria at the tender age of two. Naming our daughter after Sabine filled my heart with bittersweet emotions. I cherished the memories of my little sister, and the idea of her spirit living on through our child brought tears of both happiness and longing to my eyes. It felt like fate had intervened, granting me a chance to experience the love I had lost many years ago.

And so, on the warm summer day of June 25, 1976, Sabine was born. As I held her in my arms, I couldn't help but feel an overwhelming sense of familiarity. My little sister had been reborn, her spirit shining brightly through our daughter's eyes. Once filled with laughter and joy, our home now echoed with the pitter-patter of little feet and Sabine's infectious laugh. The nursery we had lovingly prepared became a sanctuary of dreams and imagination.

The Magical Journey of Sabine's Childhood

Betsy decided to become a full-time mother, dedicating herself wholeheartedly to raising Sabine. Witnessing the love and care she poured into our little girl filled me with admiration and gratitude. Together, we began a journey of nurturing and creating a haven of love and joy.

Once an empty piece of land boasting a magnificent backyard, our lot transformed into a beautiful garden. We poured our hearts and souls into cultivating this oasis, which became a sanctuary for Sabine's imagination to flourish. Oh, how she reveled in the simple pleasures of childhood, especially when the rains came and muddied the yard. Her laughter echoed through the air, a symphony of pure delight.

Betsy's background as a movie actor and her passion for performing in the local theater left an indelible mark on our little Sabine. At a tender age, she began to emulate her mother's grace and charm. I can still hear the rhythmic tap dancing of her tiny feet on the slate floor, a melody that resonates in my heart today. With infectious giggles, she would slip into her mother's shoes, parading around the house with a contagious sense of wonder and joy.

We believed in giving Sabine the freedom to explore her creativity, providing her with a canvas upon which she could paint her dreams. Her imagination knew no bounds, and we encouraged her every step of the way. It was a privilege to witness her blossom into a radiant soul, her spirit shining brightly as she grew and developed.

Those years were the most enchanting and cherished chapter of my life. Sabine's journey from a playful child to a remarkable young woman was a noteworthy tapestry woven with love, laughter, and countless memories. She formed lifelong friendships that stood the test of time, and her infectious passion and acceptance touched the hearts of all who knew her.

Despite her challenges, Sabine emerged as a beacon of light, radiating warmth and compassion. Her love for us runs deep, etched forever in the depths of our hearts. Our bond is unbreakable, a testament to the passion and devotion that filled our home during those magical years.

A Journey of Love and Understanding: Navigating the Challenges of Marriage

I was married to Betsy for more than eleven years. Our story, however, took a turn that led us down a path of separation and divorce in 1986. It was a difficult time for all of us, and I want my grandkids to understand the complexities of relationships, even when love is present. During the last few years of our marriage, things began to unravel. Arguments became more frequent, and Betsy seemed unhappy. I, too, felt a sense of helplessness, as if nothing I did could bring her joy. We both carried the weight of our pasts and the cultural differences that came with our upbringings. My German heritage and rigid upbringing clashed with Betsy's American background, creating unique challenges for us to navigate.

In 1985, Betsy decided to leave the marriage, taking Sabine with her. It was a heartbreaking moment for both of us. Perhaps Betsy believed that some time apart would allow us to miss each other and find a way back together. As the weeks went by, I found myself sinking into a deep depression, missing our daughter and Betsy immensely. Seeking guidance, I turned to a psychiatrist for support.

Our precious daughter, Sabine, was caught in our struggles. The judge had granted us equal joint custody, meaning that Sabine would spend one week with Betsy and the next with me. It was an arrangement that aimed to provide stability, but it was undeniably challenging for our young girl. She carried the weight of our separation on her tiny shoulders, and it broke my heart to see her so sad.

After several months of this arrangement, I decided to have a heartfelt conversation with Sabine. Regardless of the judge's decision, I wanted her to know that her happiness was my utmost priority. With tears streaming down her face, Sabine bravely expressed her desire to be with her mother. At that moment, I knew that I had to honor her wishes. I assured her that she had to let her mom know whenever she wanted to be with me, and I would pick her up.

This decision brought Sabine a sense of relief, evident in the newfound happiness she exuded. It was a difficult choice, but seeing her smile made it worthwhile. Our journey as a family had only just begun, and while our marriage had ended, our love for Sabine remained unwavering.

Over the years, Betsy and I have worked hard to maintain a healthy co-parenting relationship. We put aside our differences and focused on what was best for Sabine. As Sabine grew older, she began to understand the complexities of relationships and the challenges that can arise, even when love is abundant. We openly discussed the reasons behind our divorce, emphasizing that it was not a reflection of our love for her but rather a result of the unique circumstances we faced as a couple. Through it all, Sabine learned the importance of communication, empathy, and understanding.

Today, Sabine is a successful, compassionate, extraordinary woman. Her marriage to her college sweetheart, Jordan, has brought immense joy and become a testament to the harmonious blending of their diverse backgrounds.

Sabine, hailing from a rich German heritage, and Jordan, with a deep-rooted Jewish background, embarked on a remarkable journey of embracing both backgrounds. Their unwavering commitment to understanding and respecting each other's traditions has been inspiring. Together, they have created a nurturing environment where their children, Grace, Emery, and Ian, are encouraged to explore and appreciate the beauty of both cultures. As a parent, I couldn't be prouder of the remarkable person Sabine has become. Her unwavering compassion and dedication to her family are genuinely awe-inspiring.

As I reflect upon the beautiful chapter of my life that was my marriage to Betsy and the precious gift of our daughter Sabine, I am reminded of the profound love that once bound us together. Though our journey as a couple ended, we made sure our daughter knew that our love was real and profound. In the depths of our hearts, Betsy and I were once deeply in love, which created the foundation upon which our family was built. Sabine must understand that even though our paths diverged, the memories we created together will forever hold a special place in my heart.

Life takes unexpected turns; sometimes, those turns lead us down separate paths. But we can grow and discover our true selves in these moments of change and transition. We learn the importance of resilience and the power of forgiveness through the challenges we face. As I progress, respecting and honoring the other person is crucial, even when the road becomes rocky. By doing so, we nurture our souls and create an environment of love and understanding for our children.

Sabine, my dear daughter, I want you to know that your mother and I may have chosen different paths, but our love for you remains unwavering. Our separation does not diminish our love and care for you. Our greatest desire is to see you thrive and flourish.

Life is a tapestry woven with joy and sorrow; embracing both means that we find the strength to move forward. As you navigate your journey, remember that love is not confined to a single chapter—it is a thread that weaves its way through our lives.

May you find solace in knowing that your parents will always cherish our time as a family. Our love for you is eternal, and we will continue to support and guide you as you embark on your path. As I reflect upon the beautiful chapter of my life that was my marriage to Betsy and the precious gift of our daughter Sabine, there is one anecdote that stands out in encapsulating the essence of our adventurous spirit and the challenges we faced together. I will share it in the next chapter.

31

The Mysterious Disappearance: Losing Betsy on a Trip from Florida

We embarked on a vacation in sunny Florida. We owned a Volkswagen pop-up camper and lived life on the road, camping at various campgrounds along our travels. Little did I know this trip would become a severe event. As our vacation ended, we packed up our belongings and began the journey back home to Philadelphia. Being adventurous, we drove straight through without stopping for an overnight stay. Oh, the things we do for spontaneity! Driving through the vast expanse of Florida and Georgia took us almost the entire day. We took turns behind the wheel, navigating the winding roads in our trusty camper. Finally, on the border of Georgia and South Carolina, we stopped for a much-needed dinner break.

After satisfying our hunger, we hopped back into the camper and prepared for the rest of the journey. Sabine and Betsy changed into their cozy pajamas and settled into the double bed at the back of the camper, covered with a warm blanket. Little did I know that this innocent scene would soon become a mix-up.

Feeling energized and eager to get us home, I offered to take over the driving duties for as long as possible. We had a small gas tank in the VW camper, so we refueled every two hundred miles or so. After the third fill-up, I pulled into another gas station in North Carolina. I exited the driver's side and opened the fuel cap at the back of the camper. As I filled the tank, I did not notice a beeping sound or a light coming from inside the camper, which would have alerted me and shown that the sliding door on the passenger side had been opened.

As I glanced back, I thought I saw Sabine and Betsy still sound asleep under the blanket and among all the pillows, and I felt confident in my ability to keep driving. So, I made the fateful decision not to wake them up. Little did I know that this decision would lead to a series of events. I quickly returned to the road, driving through the night until daybreak. I continued driving with my bulky headphones on, lost in my world of prerecorded music. Suddenly, I felt a tapping on my headphones and turned to see my daughter, Sabine, by my side. Startled, I removed the headphones and listened as she asked, "Where's mommy?" My heart skipped; in a panic, I pulled the camper off the road and tried to open the locked sliding door. With the car key in hand, I unlocked it, only to discover that Betsy was not inside. Confusion and worry consumed me. How could she have disappeared without me noticing?

Frantically, I racked my brain, trying to retrace our steps. I remembered stopping at gas stations in North and South Carolina, but I couldn't recall exactly where. I hadn't kept the receipts. Finally, I realized she must have climbed over the passenger side seat and exited the passenger side door to bypass the alert system to avoid waking Sabine up. If she had gotten out of the sliding door, she would have activated the alert system, and I would have known she got out of the camper. In those days, mobile phones were a rare luxury. My only means of communication was my trusty CB radio.

With desperation and hope, I reached out to anyone listening, sharing my predicament. Finally, a voice crackled through the CB radio, offering help. A kind stranger offered to contact the State Police. As I anxiously awaited the

State Police, my mind created wild scenarios. Had Betsy somehow escaped the camper in her pajamas, wandering the streets of an unfamiliar town? The thought sent shivers down my spine. I hoped someone might remember seeing a woman wandering the highway in pajamas. It was a long shot, but it was all I had. As time passed, my anxiety increased, but so did my resolve, and I embarked on a quest to find my missing wife. No matter how absurd the situation seemed, I refused to give up on finding Betsy.

The Great Howard Johnson's Restaurant Rescue

As fate would have it, just as I was wallowing in despair, two state police cars pulled up behind me. Bless their hearts, the officers were sympathetic and found the situation uproariously funny when I explained what had happened. With a twinkle in their eyes, they immediately released a bulletin over the police scanner, broadcasting the tale of the missing wife and the Howard Johnson's Restaurant connection to all the truckers out there.

It didn't take long for the first reply to come in. A trucker on I-95 going north had spotted a lady standing close to an exit ramp in North Carolina. He wasn't entirely sure, but he recalled seeing a Howard Johnson restaurant nearby. The state police wasted no time and immediately contacted every Howard Johnson restaurant along the I-95 corridor. It was like a scene out of a Hollywood blockbuster, with the police mobilizing their forces to rescue my dear wife. And then, like a miracle, a second trucker call came in over the scanner. Another vigilant trucker had spotted a woman at Howard Johnson's who matched my wife's description.

The excitement was palpable as the police dispatcher swiftly contacted the restaurant. They confirmed Betsy was safe and sound and cared for by the kind staff. With a sigh of relief, the state police provided me with the exit number of the Howard Johnson's. Though exhausted, I mustered every ounce of energy I had left and turned my trusty camper around, determined to reunite with my wife. The journey back on I-95 felt like an eternity, but after nearly four grueling hours, I finally arrived at Howard Johnson's.

And so, my friends, that's how the Great Howard Johnson's Restaurant Rescue unfolded. It may not have been the smoothest of our journeys, but it certainly was one for the books. The Great Howard Johnson's Restaurant Rescue became a legendary tale among our friends and family, and they would retell the story at countless gatherings for years to come. Betsy and I learned to laugh about the incident as time passed, even if she still held a grudge deep down. We realized that sometimes the most absurd and unexpected situations can bring us closer together, reminding us of the importance of communication and understanding in a relationship.

From that day forward, we agreed to always double-check before exiting any vehicle. We promised to communicate our intentions clearly, ensuring that misadventures like the Great Howard Johnson Restaurant Rescue would never occur again. And that's how a straightforward journey transformed into a crazy pursuit, teaching us about the significance of humor, forgiveness, and the influence of an exciting story. It may not have been the smoothest journey, but it was certainly one that we will never forget.

So, the next time you find yourself on a road trip, remember our tale and take a moment to appreciate the unexpected twists and turns that life throws your way. After all, these moments that create stories will make you smile and remind you of the joy that can be found in even the most challenging situations.

32

A Night of Magic and Love: Dancing Away the Blues

After Betsy's heart-wrenching departure Betsy and Sabine, I found myself lost in a sea of despair. The weight of my depression was suffocating, and I sought solace in the guidance of a psychiatrist. Months passed, and I felt like a shell of my former self.

One sunny Saturday afternoon, as I returned home from a therapy session, I stumbled upon a sight that would forever change my life. In my garden, basking in the sun's warm rays, was Sharon, my tenant. I had been renting out the first floor of my house to her and her fiancé for the past six months, but little did I know that their relationship had recently ended. In a moment of vulnerability, I shared with Sharon the depths of my depression, explaining how my therapist had suggested going out dancing to heal. To my surprise, with a sparkle in her eyes, she responded, "If you don't mind, I'd love to go dancing with you." Excitement and nerves coursed through my veins as the evening approached. Sharon was undeniably beautiful, and the fact that she was fifteen years my junior only added to my anticipation and nervousness. Determined to make this night unforgettable, I took her to Pulsations Nightclub in Glen Mills, Pennsylvania.

Pulsations was renowned for its vibrant atmosphere and energetic nightlife. It has earned a fabulous reputation since its opening in the early 1980s. The pulsating beats and dazzling lights enveloped us the moment we stepped inside, casting away any remnants of sadness that lingered within. But what truly set Pulsations apart was its pièce de résistance: a custom-built robot named Pulsar. Every night, Pulsar would emerge from a spaceship suspended above the dance floor, captivating the crowd with its mesmerizing moves. An impressive twenty-seven feet in diameter, the spaceship boasted seventy lighting systems and pulled an astonishing six hundred amps. As it descended, dry ice fog would spill out, creating an otherworldly ambiance reminiscent of a "Close Encounter of the Third Kind" scene.

Sharon and I immersed ourselves in a whirlwind of music, laughter, and newfound connection as the night unfolded. It turned out that Sharon was passionate about dancing, just like me. We moved together effortlessly on the dance floor, our bodies swaying to the rhythm of the music. The crowd's energy and pulsating beats seemed to wash away all our worries and sorrows. We laughed and talked, getting to know each other more deeply. It felt like we had known each other for years despite our brief encounters as landlord and tenant. We shared stories, dreams, and even our fears, finding solace in each other's company. My depression seemed to lessen as a newfound sense of happiness and hope took its place.

While the night eventually ended, we knew our journey was just beginning. As we said our goodbyes, promising to meet again soon, I couldn't help but feel a sense of gratitude. Amid my darkest days, a chance encounter brought light back into my life. Dancing away the blues had healed my heart and opened the door to a love I never thought possible. And so, with a renewed sense of purpose and a heart full of hope, I embarked on a new chapter of my life, ready to embrace the magic and love that awaited me.

Sharon and I eventually moved in together. Sharon, born in Germany, had a unique upbringing because of her father's military service. When his tour of duty ended, they moved back to America, where Sharon grew up. However, our love story wasn't without its challenges. One of the biggest hurdles we faced was the age difference. Naturally, Sharon's parents were initially concerned about our relationship. They worried about whether we would be compatible and how we would navigate life together. Despite their reservations, we persevered and worked hard to prove our love was genuine.

Over time, Sharon's parents accepted me into their family. We visited often and indulged in her mother's delicious German cooking. I still remember the first time I sat at their dinner table, a memorable evening filled with laughter and warmth. During that dinner, mobile phones had not yet been invented, but my company had given me a beeper, which I was wearing. As fate would have it, the beeper suddenly went off during our delightful meal, beeping loudly. With a puzzled expression, Sharon's mother asked what the sound was. At that moment, I couldn't resist injecting a little humor into the situation.

With a deadpan face, I jokingly told her it was my heart pacemaker, sensing trouble with my heart. The look of shock and concern on her face was priceless. It was enough that I was fifteen years older, but now she believed I had a pacemaker. It took a few seconds of suspense before I burst into laughter, reassuring her it was just a harmless pager from work. That lighthearted moment broke the ice and brought us all closer together. Their initial concerns melted away, replaced by genuine affection and acceptance.

33

From Love to Success: A Serendipitous Journey

During a whirlwind romance with the enchanting Sharon, my career at the American Automobile Association was soaring to new heights. I was on a steep trajectory as an IT professional, driven by passion and tenacity. Little did I know that fate had something extraordinary in store for me.

AAA had grand plans to construct a state-of-the-art data center, and to my astonishment, they chose me to lead this monumental endeavor. With this promotion came the prestigious title of CIO (chief information officer), and my new office was to be in the executive suite on the upper floor. It was a dream come true, a testament to my hard work and expertise. But of course, this new role came with its own set of challenges.

One of my first responsibilities was to assemble a team, including a personal secretary who would be my right hand in this ambitious venture. Finding the perfect secretary proved to be a daunting task. The club had a specific requirement: fluency in German and extensive secretarial experience. After a series of disappointing interviews, just as hope waned, a call from the personnel office brought a glimmer of excitement. They believed they had found the ideal candidate and promptly arranged an interview. Imagine my surprise when, as the door swung open, I laid eyes on none other than Sharon herself. I had to conceal my astonishment, for she had applied for the position. We proceeded with the interview, and as we conversed, it became abundantly clear that Sharon possessed all the qualities I sought in a secretary. Her intelligence, wit, and unwavering support for my aspirations were undeniable.

Without hesitation, I gave the personnel office my enthusiastic approval to offer Sharon the job. The thrill of having her by my side, not only as my partner in love but also as my trusted professional confidant, was immeasurable. I knew deep down that this unexpected turn of events would only strengthen our bond and propel us toward even greater success. Together, we embarked on a journey that surpassed all expectations. Sharon's fluency in German proved invaluable as we navigated collaborations and partnerships that would shape the future of AAA.

Her secretarial prowess was unmatched. She effortlessly managed my schedule, organized meetings, and ensured that every aspect of our operations ran smoothly. As time went on, our love for each other grew more robust, mirroring the success we achieved in our professional lives. We became an unstoppable force, a dynamic duo that inspired awe and admiration among our colleagues. The data center project flourished under our leadership, surpassing all benchmarks and setting new standards for the company.

But it wasn't just about the accolades and achievements. We created countless memories during our journey, both inside and outside the office. We frequently worked into the night because of our mutual passion and unwavering dedication, and these late nights turned into impromptu dance parties as we celebrated our accomplishments, big and small. Sharon's contagious laughter filled the room. As the years went by, our success continued to soar. The Automobile Club became a beacon of innovation and excellence, and we were at the forefront. Our love story intertwined with our professional triumphs, creating a narrative that was as inspiring as it was extraordinary. Looking back, it's clear that fate had a hand in bringing Sharon into my life, not just as my partner, but as my ultimate source of inspiration. Together, we defied expectations, shattered glass ceilings, and proved that love and success can coexist harmoniously.

34

A Vibrant Journey Through Our German Heritage

Life wasn't just about work for us. We are deeply connected to our German roots, which has influenced our social lives. Our love for our heritage immersed us in the German community, and we attended various events organized by German and Austrian societies in the Philadelphia area.

One of our favorite annual traditions was Oktoberfest, where we indulged in delicious German cuisine, danced to lively music, and reveled in the joyous atmosphere. We also eagerly anticipated my mother's Hamburger Abend (Evening), which allowed us to celebrate our culture with other enthusiasts. The Christmas Bazaar at the German Society was a magical affair filled with enchanting decorations, delightful treats, and heartwarming melodies. We would spend hours browsing the stalls, searching for unique gifts and savoring the festive spirit.

One highlight of our social calendar was the Fasching (Costume) Ball. We would spend weeks meticulously planning our costumes, aiming to outdo ourselves each year. The event's excitement, vibrant masks, lively music, and energetic dancing always left us with unforgettable memories. As the clock struck midnight on New Year's Eve, we would raise our glasses, toasting new beginnings and cherishing the love we shared. The Steuben Parade was a grand celebration that allowed us to proudly display our roots and honor our German-American ancestors. And, of course, we couldn't forget the German Beer Fest. These lively gatherings were a testament to our love for good company, great beer, and hearty laughter. With our friends by our sides, we would savor the celebration while exchanging tales and forging enduring bonds.

Despite the fifteen-year age difference between us, Sharon's youthful spirit kept me energized and engaged. Her beauty was undeniable, and it was no surprise when she took part in the German Beauty Contest, vying for the German Kornflower Konigen (Cornflower Queen) title. Although she didn't win the coveted title, the judges crowned her a princess, acknowledging her grace and charm. As a princess, Sharon had newfound responsibilities. She was required to attend many German affairs, make speeches, and represent the German community gracefully and elegantly.

While she initially felt hesitant about these obligations, I reassured her that she had the charisma and poise to excel in her role. Sharon embraced her new position with determination and grace. She went to charity events and supported various community initiatives, attending German festivals and connecting with people who shared our love for our heritage. Sharon's presence always added a touch of elegance to these gatherings, and I couldn't have been prouder to have her by my side.

35

Melodies of the Heart: Sharon's Musical Journey

Since she was a young girl, Sharon's fingers danced effortlessly across the ivory keys of a piano to create enchanting melodies. Music held a special place in her life, and her parents believed it was essential for her to learn the piano.

However, there was a time when Sharon resented this, for her parents would often showcase her talent like a prized possession whenever guests visited their home. It made her feel like a mere show doll, and she longed for freedom and self-expression. Our cozy living room had an old upright piano that held a treasure trove of emotions within its wooden frame. I adored those moments when Sharon would immerse herself in practice or perform a piece she had mastered.

Among all the melodies she played, my heart found solace in her passionate rendition of Beethoven's timeless masterpiece "Fur Elise." How she breathed life into every note would melt even the coldest hearts. Sometimes, when the weight of a minor disagreement lingered between us, Sharon would gracefully glide her fingers across the keys, conjuring the enchanting harmonies of "Fur Elise." In those moments, the music acted as a soothing balm, melting away any lingering tension, and I couldn't help but surrender to the power of her art.

Sharon's love for music intertwined with the festive spirit as Christmas approached. She devoted herself to rehearsing a delightful selection of classic German and American Christmas songs. With each passing day, her dedication illuminated our home, transforming it into a sanctuary of holiday cheer. The pinnacle of this magical season was the cherished Christmas Eve dinner, where Sharon's parents and my mother gathered. In the warmth and love that filled the room, Sharon would grace us with a breathtaking performance, playing a medley of Christmas songs. From the traditional melodies of Germany to the beloved tunes of America, her nimble fingers would weave a tapestry of joy, filling our hearts with the true essence of the season. Through the piano, she found her voice, and her melodies continue to resonate within my heart, forever reminding me of the magic of music.

36

Love, Sacrifice, and Dreams: A Journey of Family and Entrepreneurship

In the whirlwind of our professional success at the American Automobile Association, Sharon and I faced a unique challenge in our personal lives. As I took on the role of CIO with Sharon as my dedicated secretary, we also had to navigate the delicate balance of blending our families. I had my beautiful ten-year-old daughter Sabine, who lived with her mother, Betsy.

Sharon, never before married and having no children of her own, was stepping into the role of stepmother to Sabine. It was daunting, but Sharon's unwavering love and determination shone through as she embraced this new chapter in our lives. I watched in awe as she tirelessly worked to be Sabine's stepmother and guiding friend. It was no easy feat for a young woman like Sharon to suddenly find herself in the position of helping me raise my beloved daughter. But she faced the challenge head-on, pouring her heart and soul into creating a loving and nurturing environment for Sabine.

As we balanced our personal and professional lives, Sharon had a brilliant idea to bring us closer as a family and ignite our entrepreneurial spirits. We owned an empty lot in the picturesque Pocono Mountains of Newfoundland, Pennsylvania. Sharon saw the potential in this untouched piece of land and proposed that we turn it into something extraordinary. With her boundless creativity and my unwavering support, we embarked on a journey to transform the empty lot into a beautiful vacation home. Together, we envisioned a beautiful retreat, a haven where we could escape the hustle and bustle of everyday life and immerse ourselves in nature's beauty.

We poured our hearts and souls into this project, working tirelessly to bring our dream to life. Sharon's eye for design and attention to detail ensured that every aspect of the new vacation home in the Pocono Springs Estate exuded elegance and charm. From the breathtaking landscapes to the meticulously curated interiors, our retreat became a sanctuary for those seeking solace and rejuvenation.

But beyond the success of this venture, the accurate measure of our journey lay in the love and sacrifice we made for each other. Sharon's unwavering commitment to being a stepmother to Sabine was nothing short of extraordinary. She embraced the role with open arms, showering Sabine with love, guidance, and support. I couldn't be happier about the sacrifices Sharon made to help me be the best father I could be. She put her desires and dreams on hold to ensure our family remained united. Looking back on our journey, it's clear that love, sacrifice, and dreams can intertwine in the most beautiful and unexpected ways.

37

A Journey of Love and Friendship

As I reminisce about the beautiful moments I shared with my beloved Sharon, I am overwhelmed with profound gratitude. Like any other, our love story had its difficulties, but it was an incredible journey that shaped me into the person I am today.

Our marriage ties and shared German heritage bound Sharon and me together. A delightful synchrony brought us closer, nurturing a profound understanding. Her unwavering support and inspiration became the fuel that propelled me forward in my career at AAA. With Sharon by my side, I felt invincible, ready to conquer any challenge that came my way.

Yet, life has a way of surprising us: One day, Sharon expressed her desire to part ways, leaving me bewildered and with a heavy heart. It was a challenging moment, and I couldn't help but ponder the reasons behind this sudden change. Perhaps the fifteen-year age difference had cast a shadow of uncertainty over her future with me. Or maybe there were other intricate layers to her decision that I failed to comprehend fully. Regardless, I accepted her choice with a heavy heart, respecting her need for a different path.

Though the conclusion of our chapter as a married couple left me longing, I am eternally thankful for the time we spent together. Our love was a gift, an experience that shaped me profoundly. It reminded me of the beauty of cherishing every moment, showing that life's tapestry is made up of both joy and sorrow.

In the aftermath of our separation, a remarkable transformation occurred. Despite the end of our romantic relationship, Sharon and I discovered the immense strength of our friendship. We navigated the intricate maze of emotions, emerging on the other side with an unbreakable bond. Today, we remain friends, supporting each other through life's twists and turns and cherishing the memories we created as partners. I stand here today with a heart overflowing with gratitude, not regret. Sharon, my dear friend, I appreciate your presence in my life. You motivate me to pursue my dreams and remind me that love can manifest in different ways.

38

Retirement: Embracing Change and Paving the Way

As I reflect on my time at AAA, I can't help but feel a sense of pride and accomplishment. It was an era of immense growth and transformation, both for the organization and me. I joined the IT department in 1970, and little did I know that this would mark the beginning of an extraordinary chapter in my life.

AAA was undergoing a remarkable consolidation process during this period. We witnessed a significant reduction from a network of 114 independent clubs to just forty-three. It was a time of change, challenges, and opportunities. Among these transformations, AAA Mid-Atlantic, the club I had the privilege to work for, embarked on several large-scale acquisitions, the most recent being the Maryland Club.

Each merger brought its own set of hurdles, particularly regarding staff duplication. The Maryland Club had a vibrant and youthful IT team. As someone in my fifties, I couldn't help but notice the rapid advancements in technology and the ease with which the younger generation embraced them. I wondered if my age could hinder my ability to keep up with the ever-evolving tech landscape.

Recognizing the writing on the wall, I quietly devised a plan to secure my future and ensure a smooth transition for the IT department. I proposed an early retirement to the company, outlining a comprehensive package to benefit both parties involved. I would retire at fifty-two with a fully defined pension payout at fifty-five. I negotiated for full medical benefits until the end of my days and the opportunity to work as a consultant for AAA, guaranteeing a set number of hours each week at a predetermined rate for the three years until my pension kicked in.

The proposal sparked intense discussions as AAA weighed the potential loss of my experience and expertise against the need for a younger, more tech-savvy workforce. Ultimately, they accepted my offer, recognizing the value of a smooth transition and the importance of embracing the future.

And so, at fifty-two, I bid farewell to my role as CIO. It was a bittersweet moment as I left behind a position that had brought me immense joy and fulfillment. But I knew this decision would pave the way for a new generation of IT professionals to lead AAA. During my consulting years, I witnessed incredible technological advancements and their impact on the automobile industry. From the rise of online services to the emergence of mobile applications, the world was becoming increasingly interconnected. The start of my pension at fifty-five was a milestone that marked the end of one chapter and the beginning of another.

Reflecting on my time at AAA, I am filled with pride and accomplishment. I had the privilege of witnessing the organization's transformation from a network of independent clubs to a merged force, ready to tackle the challenges of the modern world. My decision to embrace change and pave the way for a new generation of IT professionals was a testament to my adaptability and foresight. Today, as I enjoy my well-deserved retirement, I take pride in knowing that I played a part in AAA's success story. My time as a CIO will always remind me of the power of embracing change and the importance of staying ahead of the curve.

As I closed this chapter of my life, I looked forward to the fresh adventures that awaited me. While retirement may mark the end of one's professional journey, it opens the door to a world of possibilities and new beginnings. I am grateful for the experiences, the friendships, and the lessons learned along the way. Reaching new heights as CIO at AAA was just the beginning of an extraordinary life filled with purpose and fulfillment.

39

Embracing Freedom: Adventures in the Late 1990s

As the end of the 20th century approached, I experienced newfound freedom and endless possibilities. In my mid-fifties and having experienced many ups and downs, I found myself single, twice divorced, and filled with a renewed energy and eagerness to explore this new chapter.

One of my favorite pastimes during this exciting era was venturing into Philadelphia's vibrant nightclubs on weekend evenings. The club scene in the late 1990s was a melting pot of music, dance, and camaraderie. It was a place where people of all ages and backgrounds came together to let loose and enjoy the rhythm of life.

Swing dancing had taken the world by storm, and I couldn't resist joining in on the fun. I took swing dance lessons, immersing myself in the lively and energetic movements that characterized this popular dance style. The joy of swing dancing was infectious, and I twirled and spun on the dance floor, lost in the rhythm and laughter of the moment. It was a time of pure bliss and carefree abandon.

But my adventures didn't stop there. In-line skating had also become a sensation, replacing traditional roller skating as a go-to activity for those seeking an adrenaline rush. I eagerly embraced this new hobby, strapping on my in-line skate and hitting the pavement with exhilaration. Yes, I may have gained a fair share of bruises along the way, but they were badges of honor, reminders of the daring spirit that fueled my newfound zest for life.

This period also saw the rise of in-line skating rings popping up in various locations across the city. Enthusiasts gathered at these vibrant hubs, forging friendships and making memories. I met a diverse group of individuals who shared my love for the sport, and together we explored the city's streets and parks, gliding effortlessly through the urban landscape.

I was experiencing fun and energy that I hadn't felt in years. It was a time of liberation, where age became nothing more than a number, and the possibilities seemed endless. I felt young again, embracing the freedom to pursue new hobbies, make new connections, and live life to the fullest.

Reflecting on those exhilarating years, I am reminded of the power of embracing change and stepping outside one's comfort zone. The late 1990s were a testament to the resilience of the human spirit and the joy of embracing new experiences. It was a time of personal growth and self-discovery where I learned to relinquish societal expectations and live on my terms.

The club scene and swing dancing allowed me to express myself freely, let the music guide my movements, and connect with others on a deeper level. The dance floor's energy was infectious, and I found solace in the rhythm and connection that came with each step. It served as a reminder that age is irrelevant and a youthful spirit is always within us.

In-line skating also brought a sense of adventure and thrill to my days. The wind in my hair and the smooth glide of the wheels beneath my feet gave me pure freedom. The skating rings that dotted the city became playgrounds where I could challenge myself, meet like-minded individuals, and revel in the simple joy of movement.

But beyond the physical activities, the late 1990s were a time of personal transformation, self-reflection, and introspection when I learned to embrace my desires and passions without fear of judgment. I discovered the importance of self-care, self-love, and the power of a positive attitude.

As the years went by, the memories of those vibrant nights at the clubs and exhilarating skating adventures became cherished moments in my life. They were a powerful reminder that joy and fulfillment are unlimited, regardless of age.

40

From Vacation Home to Spiritual Shenanigans: The Pocono Chronicles

As the 21st century began and I entered my early sixties, I felt a burning desire to reinvent myself and try something completely different. Little did I know that this decision would lead to a hilarious and unexpected turn of events. With a stroke of genius (or perhaps madness), I made the audacious choice to live full time in our beautiful four-bedroom Pocono house and open it up to guests. This was before the days of Airbnb, so I was indeed a pioneer in unconventional hospitality.

Now, here's where things get delightfully peculiar. I wanted to transform our rustic retreat into a spiritual one, but truth be told, I had no clear vision of what that meant. It just sounded good to me, like a whimsical notion that might change lives. And so, armed with enthusiasm but essentially clueless, I set out on this peculiar path. But fate had a funny way of intervening. Back in the day, I had taken part in a self-improvement workshop called "The Landmark Forum." Little did I know this workshop would play a pivotal role in the zany tale that was about to unfold.

One fine day, the phone rang as I was basking in the tranquility of my Pocono retreat. It was Fred, a fellow workshop participant who also lived in the

Pocono Mountains. Fred was like a character from a storybook: a simple mountain guy who had spent an entire year living in the woods like a hermit, surviving off the land. His tales of adventure and survival were nothing short of captivating. As fate would have it, he had heard through the grapevine that I had moved to the Poconos, and he was eager to reconnect. Fred's eyes lit up like a campfire on a starry night when I shared my wild idea of turning my home into a spiritual retreat. He was ready to embark on this whimsical journey with me.

Together, we hatched a plan. I would take care of entertaining and nurturing our guests within the cozy confines of our Pocono house, while Fred would take them on thrilling adventure hikes, teaching them the ways of nature and survival skills. It was a match made in eccentric heaven. With our roles defined and our enthusiasm soaring, we set out to make our dream a reality. We even went as far as creating a promotional video to spread the word about our spiritual shenanigans. Believe it or not, it worked! Within three months, we welcomed our first batch of curious guests, and our serene sanctuary was bursting at the seams with laughter, enlightenment, and a touch of madness. As the guests arrived, we could sense their excitement and anticipation. They had come seeking a spiritual retreat, but little did they know they were starting a journey filled with laughter, unexpected challenges, and many of nature's wonders.

With his rugged charm and wild spirit, Fred led our guests on exhilarating hikes through the untamed wilderness of the Pocono Mountains. He taught them how to identify edible plants, build makeshift shelters, and communicate with squirrels (yes, you read that right!). His wealth of knowledge astounded our guests, and his contagious enthusiasm could not help but sweep them away.

Meanwhile, back at the house, I played the role of the spiritual guide, leading our guests through meditation sessions that were occasionally interrupted by the sound of Fred's triumphant whoops echoing through the trees. The occasional squirrel would scamper across the windowsill and appear eager to join our philosophical musings as we dove into lengthy discussions about the meaning of life. Our guests were diverse, with unique stories and reasons for seeking a spiritual retreat. But what united them all was the laughter that filled the air. This camaraderie blossomed through chaos and the unforgettable memories forged in the heart of the Pocono Mountains.

41

Journey to the Center of Hilarity: The Shaman's Shenanigans

With our Pocono retreat thriving and guests flocking to experience our spiritual shenanigans, Fred and I knew it was time to take things to the next level. Emboldened by our success, we brought in a mystical element that would take our guests on a journey they would never forget. Enter the enigmatic shaman, known by her spiritual name, "Guru Gecko." With her flowing robes and a twinkle in her eye, she exuded an aura of wisdom and mystery. We knew she was the missing piece to our whimsical puzzle.

Guru Gecko had a special talent for guiding people on spiritual journeys, and she had a unique plan for our guests. We were about to embark on a trip to the center of the earth, a journey that would test our imaginations and push the boundaries of reality. But first, we needed to embrace our spiritual identities. Fred became "Wondering Deer," a name that perfectly captured his adventurous spirit and his knack for wandering through life with a twinkle in his eye. I became "Laughing Deer," a name that reflected my love for laughter and my ability to find joy in even the most absurd situations. And so, armed with our newfound spiritual names, we invited our guests to join us on this extraordinary expedition. But there was a catch: They had to develop spiritual names that genuinely captured their unique personalities. The results were nothing short of hilarious.

We gathered around a bonfire, the flames dancing in rhythm with excitement. Holding hands, we chanted and shared drinks to loosen our spirits. And then, it was time for Guru Gecko to lead us to the earth's center. She transported us to a realm where reality and imagination intertwined with her mystical incantations and a sprinkle of fairy dust (okay, maybe it was just glitter). It was a journey like no other, filled with fantastical creatures, talking trees, and even a dance-off with a mischievous gnome.

Our minds expanded as we delved deeper into the earth's core, and our laughter echoed through the caverns. We shared our wildest imaginings, creating a tapestry of absurdity that left us gasping for breath between fits of giggles. One guest, who had a penchant for puns, became a "Whimsical Wordplay Wizard." Another, with a love for all things sparkly, transformed into a "Glittering Unicorn Queen." And let's not forget about "Adventurous Squirrel Whisperer," who had a knack for communicating with our furry woodland friends. The journey to the earth's center was a whirlwind of laughter, enlightenment, and downright silliness. We encountered mystical creatures who taught us the art of interpretive dance, discovered hidden treasure troves of wisdom buried deep within the Earth's core, and even had a friendly debate with a talking rock about the meaning of life (spoiler alert: the rock won).

But perhaps the most memorable moment was when we stumbled upon a secret disco party hosted by a group of dancing gnomes. We joined the festivities, busting out our best moves and laughing until our sides ached. It was a sight to behold—a group of spiritual seekers letting loose and embracing the sheer joy of being alive. We were forever changed as we emerged from our journey to the center of hilarity. Our hearts were lighter, our spirits lifted, and our laughter echoed through the Pocono Mountains.

42

Unleashing the Magic Touch

We realized our Pocono retreat was missing one crucial element: a massage therapist. Guru Gecko suggested that I, yes, yours truly, take a crash course in massage therapy and become the resident masseur.

Now, the thought of me, a self-proclaimed spiritual guide and adventurer, donning a pair of silky shorts and giving massages was hilarious and slightly terrifying. But life is all about embracing the unexpected, right? And so, with excitement and trepidation, I agreed to become the Pocono Mountains' most unconventional masseur.

Guru Gecko wasted no time in giving me a crash course in the art of massage. Picture this: me, lying on the dining room table in nothing but my shorts, surrounded by candles and the soothing sounds of spiritual music. It was a sight to behold, and I couldn't help but chuckle at the absurdity of it all. As Guru Gecko guided me and showed me the proper techniques and pressure points, I couldn't help but wonder if I had what it took to pull this off. Buoyed by her confidence in my abilities, I gave it my all and embraced this new adventure.

And so, we set up the massage table, ready to welcome our first guest. Clad in a luxurious, silky bathrobe, I prepared myself for the task. The soft glow of candlelight filled the room, creating an atmosphere of tranquility and relaxation. As the guest lay down on the table, I took a deep breath and let my hands work their magic. With each stroke and knead, I channeled my inner masseur, tapping into a newfound talent I never knew I possessed. And to my surprise, I was a hit! The guest melted into bliss, their worries and stress melting under my touch. It was as if I had unlocked a hidden talent, a secret power that brought joy and relaxation to those in need. Who would have thought the spiritual guide and adventurer would become the Pocono Mountains' most sought-after masseur?

As the weeks passed, I honed my skills, experimenting with different techniques and even incorporating a touch of whimsy into my massages. I would sprinkle a pinch of fairy dust (okay, maybe it was just scented oil) onto my hands before each session, creating an enchanting aroma that transported our guests to a realm of pure relaxation. But it wasn't just the massages that made them smile. The entire experience included the candlelit room, the soothing music, and the occasional burst of laughter that echoed through the walls. We had created a sanctuary of silliness where laughter and relaxation intertwined most delightfully. My magical messages spread like wildfire, and soon, guests eager to experience the healing touch of the Pocono Mountains' most unconventional masseur booked our retreat solid.

People came from far and wide, seeking solace from the chaos of everyday life and leaving with a renewed sense of joy and tranquility. But it was one guest's request for a massage and interpretive dance that may have made for the most memorable massage session.

Yes, you read that correctly: interpretive dance. And being an adventurous soul, I couldn't resist the opportunity to combine two of my newfound talents. As the guests lay on the massage table, I moved around them, gracefully swaying and twirling to the rhythm of the music. My hands danced across their bodies, mirroring the movements of my body, creating a symphony of relaxation and whimsy. It was a sight to behold, and the guest couldn't help but giggle with delight.

43

The Hilarious Mayan Chocolate Adventure

Fred, the "Wondering Deer," stumbled upon a bag of magic mushrooms from a Mexican maintenance worker. Little did he know this chance encounter would lead to a wild and hilarious escapade. With mischievous glee, Fred hatched a brilliant plan to create a special Mayan chocolate infused with a touch of magic mushrooms.

Gathering our supplies, we embarked on a quest to bring laughter and delight to all who dared to taste our concoction. First, we acquired many cases of empty canning jars, each adorned with a whimsical Mayan motif. As I, the "Smiling Deer," meticulously painted each jar, they transformed into vibrant vessels of enchantment. Next, we bought a whopping ten pounds of block chocolate, which Fred, the master of culinary chaos, gleefully ground into tiny chips. With a mischievous glint in our eyes, we combined the fine chocolate with just a hint of magic mushroom, careful not to go overboard, and a medley of herbs and spices. Behold, the finished product was born!

Eager to test our creation, I brewed the first batch of hot chocolate, and with hearts pounding in anticipation, we embarked on another daring spiritual adventure to the center of the earth, a journey filled with unexpected twists and turns. Oh, the laughter that echoed through the cavernous depths! We couldn't help but giggle uncontrollably, knowing that our guests would experience the same joy and relaxation. As we emerged from our underground expedition, we carried the secret to a truly unforgettable hot chocolate experience. Each sip of the magical blend of Mayan chocolate and a touch of whimsy would transport our guests to joy and merriment, lifting their spirits. And so, dear friends, our spiritual retreat adventure ended, leaving behind a trail of laughter and a legacy of unforgettable memories. The "Hilarious Mayan Chocolate Adventure" tale would endure through generations, proving the influence of imagination, friendship, and joy in the most unexpected places.

44

Embracing Family Ties: A Quest for Connection

In the late 1990s, I embarked on a journey of self-discovery that uncovered untold stories of my extended American family. This voyage of connecting my mother's relatives from across the ocean became a chapter of my life filled with anticipation and excitement.

Among the cherished members of my American kin were Uncle Werner and his wife, Sandy. They were the epitome of warmth and acceptance, treating me as one of their own. Uncle Werner Sr., Sandy's father, shared a familial connection with my mother, further deepening the bond between our families. Their unwavering love and support brought me a sense of belonging that I had never experienced before. Every invitation to their family gatherings and events felt like a heartfelt embrace, enveloping me in a world where I felt part of something greater.

Their children (Eric, Kirsten, and Kelly) and their children's spouses, (Lisa, Nick, and Dennis) created an atmosphere filled with contagious laughter and joy. Together, we created unforgettable memories, forever holding a special place in my heart. Their genuine love and affection made me realize the power of family connections extending beyond bloodlines. Through their embrace,

I discovered the beauty of a larger family unit that transcended borders and cultures. My relationship with my American family has given me a newfound appreciation for the value of love, belonging, and the satisfaction of being a part of something bigger than myself, besides a deeper understanding of my heritage.

My American Family Clan

Uncle Werner Sr. is shrouded in mystery and wisdom. He and Emmy, my maternal grandmother with a spirited soul, are siblings. Uncle Werner Sr. is a man of stature who loved his family. His son, Werner Jr., and his lovely wife, Sandy, have three exceptional children—Eric, Kelly, and Kirsten, my second cousins.

Eric, the dashing gentleman of the trio, has found his soulmate in the enchanting Lisa. Their love story, a tale of passion and companionship, adds another layer of richness to our ever-expanding family saga. As the saying goes, opposites attract. This couldn't be more accurate for Eric and Lisa. They're not only intelligent and successful, but also a source of entertainment.

Eric is the epitome of laid back. Whenever we get together, it's like the world slows down. I love to hang out with him and take a few shots of Jägermeister. It's as if he has a PhD in relaxation. If I ever need a therapist, Eric is my go-to guy. He's got this magical aura that makes you want to kick back and forget your worries.

And then there's Lisa—a force to be reckoned with! She's the definition of a strong woman, and I can't help but admire her. I've told her that when I kick the bucket (which hopefully won't be soon), she must deliver the eulogy at my funeral. I know she'll make everyone laugh and cry simultaneously.

Kelly, the enthusiastic member of this captivating trio of cousins, has joined forces with her beloved Dennis, a gentle giant. From the moment we met, there was an undeniable bond between us. She would greet me with a grin as wide as the Grand Canyon and a hug that could rival a bear's embrace. She had this unique way of calling me "Cousin Hans," which always made me chuckle. We filled our time together with an endless stream of laughter and unforgettable moments. But what set us apart was our shared love for dancing. She had an infinite arsenal of moves. She led the way to the dance floor with her infectious energy. My cousin Kelly was not just a cousin; she was a tornado of joy and laughter. I smile whenever I think of her.

Lastly, let me tell you about the delightful duo of Kirsten and Nick, who light up any room they enter. Kirsten is a shining star, captivating everyone with her charm, and Nick oozes charisma, melting hearts wherever he goes. Kirsten is also a diva in the most enchanting way possible. You can feel the love radiating from her when you're around her. And let me tell you, she's got some serious sex appeal, at least in my humble opinion!

Speaking of Kirsten, this hilarious little tale always comes to mind. The house that she and Nick bought had a pesky leaking roof that became the stuff of legends in our family. Every time we saw each other, the topic somehow found its way into the conversation, and that leak just wouldn't quit! It was a never-ending saga.

But the last time I saw Kirsten, she revealed that they finally discovered the source of the leak, and guess what? It was coming from the neighbor's house! After all those years of enduring that leaky roof, it turned out to be the neighbor's fault. Who would have thought? Ah, Kirsten and Nick genuinely hold a special place in my heart. Their love and loyalty are unmatched, and they always bring a smile to my face. Whether it's Kirsten's diva antics or their never-ending roof saga, they know how to keep life interesting.

I've learned to embrace the quirks and complexities of my familial connec-tions, for they form the tapestry of my unique story. In connecting with my American family, I discovered a deeper understanding of my heritage and a newfound appreciation for the power of love, belonging, and the joy of being part of something greater than myself.

Reflecting on that transformative period, I am grateful for the love and acceptance I found in Uncle Werner, Sandy, and their extraordinary children. They taught me the significance of forging meaningful connections and celebrating our ties.

45

Embracing Oma's Golden Years

When I retired at age fifty-five in 1996, a remarkable opportunity presented itself to me. Oma, my beloved mother, born in Germany in 1914, was eighty-two. Since she arrived in the United States in the late 1970s, she had dedicated herself to the German Society of Pennsylvania in Philadelphia, serving as a business agent and orchestrating social events. She had become an adored member of the Society, and all cherished her presence.

However, as fate would have it, just shortly after my retirement, I received a phone call from the president of the Society. People raised concerns about Oma's health and age, questioning her ability to continue managing society's affairs. They suggested the idea of her retiring and even proposed the notion of a nursing home. This news struck a chord within me, and I pondered the situation for days.

Ultimately, I made a decision that would forever change both our lives. I resolved to bring Oma into our home and care for her. When I shared this plan with her, she initially felt sad about leaving her cherished role behind. But the prospect of living with me quickly grew more appealing, and her excitement outweighed any reservations. Wasting no time, I transformed the first floor of my house into a cozy apartment just for Oma. It even boasted a backdoor exit that opened to a breathtaking city garden stretching to the next block. I knew this would bring her immense joy, and I couldn't help but feel a swell of pride at the opportunity to care for my mother and spend precious time with her.

Memories of the Charming Italian Market

Like clockwork, Oma would rise at eight o'clock every morning. She had a particular routine that made her feel beautiful and confident. With a little black bow tie adorning the back of her hair and a spritz of her favorite perfume, she would explore the wonders of the Philadelphia Italian market, just a block from our home. The Italian market was a treasure trove, not just for its fresh vegetables, but for its vibrant atmosphere. It was a place where bakeries, butchers, flower shops, coffee shops, bookstores, spice stores, and pizza shops all coexisted harmoniously. It was like stepping into a big family where everyone knew each other.

In no time at all, Oma had made countless friends at the market. She had a way of charming everyone she met, and they reciprocated by treating her with the utmost respect and kindness. People always allowed Oma to go ahead and never made her wait in line. It was heartwarming to witness the genuine connections she formed with the people there.

Every morning, Oma would make her way to Sarcone's Bakery, a favorite spot of hers, to pick up freshly baked Kaiser rolls—one for me and one for herself. She would also grab a copy of the *Philadelphia Inquirer*, her trusted news source. She would return home with her bounty, ready to start our day. Oma took great pleasure in preparing our breakfast. She would set the table, make the coffee, then call down to me affectionately as "Jochen," announcing that breakfast was ready. During the summer, she would arrange our breakfast table outside, allowing us to enjoy the warmth of the sun and the beauty of our garden. As we sat down to eat, Oma would delve into the crossword and puzzle sections of the newspaper while I perused the business section. It was a delightful sight, the two of us engrossed in our respective activities yet still connected by the family bond. We always had stories to share and experiences to discuss, making our breakfast together a cherished everyday ritual.

The breakfasts we shared became more than a meal; they were moments of connection and love. We would laugh, reminisce, and sometimes even debate over the crossword clues. Oma's wisdom and wit always shone through, and I treasured every word she spoke. The charm of the Italian market seemed to seep into our breakfast conversations. Oma would share stories of the colorful characters she had met, the delicious pastries she had tasted, and the vibrant energy that filled the air. It was as if the market had become an extension of our home, where we could immerse ourselves in the rich tapestry of Italian culture.

As the years passed, our breakfasts remained a constant source of joy and comfort. Oma's presence filled our home with warmth and love, and the Italian market continued to be a place of community and connection. We often invited friends and neighbors to join us, creating a lively gathering filled with laughter and good food. Looking back, I realize that those breakfasts with Oma were more than just a meal; they celebrated family, tradition, and simple pleasures. The Italian market charmed our mornings with its bustling energy and friendly faces.

46

A Serendipitous Encounter: Love Blossoms Amid Uncertainty

In the summer of 2002, a wave of excitement crashed over me as Oma and I received a coveted invitation to the graduation party of my distant cousin Susan's daughter Katie. Little did I know that this celebration would be the backdrop for a fateful meeting with my future wife, Donna.

As we arrived at the party, Oma gracefully mingled with familiar faces, effort-lessly weaving herself into conversations. Meanwhile, I made a beeline for the food table, my stomach eager to sample the delectable spread. Laughter and banter filled the air as friends and family indulged in lighthearted merriment. And there, amid the delightful chaos, stood Donna, a vision of elegance and grace. She was a close friend of my distant cousin Susan, and her slender frame moved with a gentle fluidity. My eyes were immediately drawn to her as she delicately filled her plate with various hors d'oeuvres. Unable to resist the opportunity to engage in playful banter, I playfully commented on the modest portion of food she had chosen. This lighthearted remark catalyzed our conversation, a spark that ignited the flame of our connection.

While savoring breakfast with Oma the following day, she casually mentioned inviting Cousin Susan and her friend Donna for a coffee gathering the following Saturday. I hid the fact that I had already met Donna at the party to contain my excitement. The following Saturday, as the sun bathed our beautiful garden in a warm glow, Susan and Donna arrived for an enchanting afternoon of coffee and dessert. This meeting would begin a journey filled with unexpected twists and turns, leading to a love defying all odds.

As we sat among the fragrant blossoms, laughter and joy filled the air, momentarily overshadowing the fact that Donna was still married. Despite this knowledge, our connection was undeniable, and we reveled in each other's company, cherishing every moment we shared. During this delightful gathering, I invited Donna and her husband, Jim, to join us for a grand garden party the following weekend, where our extended family would gather to celebrate life and love.

To my surprise, Jim seemed captivated by my presence, and he graciously invited me to join them on his boat, cruising along the tranquil Delaware River. I eagerly accepted. As the sun danced upon the gentle ripples of the river, we embarked on an adventure that would forever change our lives. Laughter echoed through the air as we shared stories, sipped refreshing drinks, and reveled in the sheer bliss of the moment. And through it all, my heart couldn't help but gravitate toward Donna, sensing an unspoken connection that transcended the boundaries of friendship.

Upon returning home, a wave of realization washed over me as I discovered I had inadvertently left my camera on Jim's boat. Eager to retrieve this precious memento, I reached out to them, and we agreed to meet at a bustling mall for lunch, where they would return my camera to me. Little did I know that this ordinary encounter would become a turning point in our story. To my surprise, it was Donna who arrived alone, her eyes filled with a mixture of anticipation and vulnerability. Jim's absence presented an opportunity for us to explore our connection, away from prying eyes and the constraints of societal expectations.

Over a leisurely lunch, we shared our deepest fears and desires, and Donna confided in me, revealing the crumbling state of her marriage. At that moment, our hearts beat in unison, silently acknowledging the magnetic pull that had drawn us together. The air crackled with unspoken words, and our unspoken desires hung heavy. It was as if fate had orchestrated this meeting.

As the afternoon stretched, time seemed to stand still, allowing us to explore the depths of our connection. With every word exchanged, every shared laugh, and every stolen glance, our bond grew stronger, defying the boundaries of societal norms and expectations. We were two souls entwined in a dance of forbidden love, yearning to break free from the shackles that held us back.

When the time came to bid farewell, our embraces lingered as if neither of us wanted to let go. We whispered promises of staying in touch, but in our hearts, we knew this was just the beginning of a love story that would challenge the very fabric of our lives.

Days turned into weeks and weeks into months as Donna and I navigated the treacherous waters of our emotions. We found solace in our phone calls, stolen glances, and rendezvous that only fueled the fire burning within us. Our love grew stronger each day, and we couldn't ignore the all-consuming force that fueled our desire to be together. But we faced many obstacles: The guilt of betraying Jim, the fear of societal judgment, and the uncertainty of what lay ahead weighed heavily on our hearts. But we were determined to fight for our love.

47

A Journey of Healing: Donna's Triumph Over Adversity

Donna, leaving her husband Jim and her adult children, Kirk, Brett, and Brandon, was undoubtedly one of her most challenging decisions ever. The weight of her emotions was almost unbearable as she took that first step toward a new life. The lack of support she received from her children made leaving her family behind even more painful. The wounds left by the broken marriage were deep, and the road to recovery seemed endless. However, with each passing day, Donna found solace in the minor victories she achieved. She slowly rebuilt her life, and the pain eventually subsided.

Donna was not the only one involved in this healing process. Her children also had their battles to fight. They had grown up witnessing the strain of their parents' marriage, which left an indelible mark on their hearts. However, as time passed, they understood the complexities of their parents' relationship and its toll on their mother.

Brandon, the oldest, was the first to truly comprehend the depth of his mother's pain. He had always been perceptive, noticing his father's late nights and extravagant spending at the Spinnerstown Restaurant. Brandon's empathy allowed him to see beyond the surface and understand the toll it had taken on his mother's emotional well-being. Years passed, and the wounds healed. Donna and her children slowly rebuilt their relationship, one conversation at a time. Their hearts were no longer filled with pain and resentment, but with understanding and forgiveness. They realized that life was too short to hold on to grudges, and the only way to move forward was to let go of the past.

Donna's journey was challenging, but her determination and resilience carried her through. Jim, her estranged husband, had also transformed. The tireless effort he had put into his machine shop had affected their marriage. After years of separation and personal growth, Donna and Jim were at a crossroads. They had both changed, learned from their mistakes and were ready to face the past head-on. Having realized his work's impact on their marriage, Jim attempted to prioritize his family over his business.

Donna and Jim's reconciliation was not an overnight process. It took time, patience, and a willingness to forgive and forget. They started by rebuilding their friendship, slowly rekindling the love that had once brought them together. Their children watched in awe as their parents navigated the complexities of their relationship with grace and maturity. Donna's and Jim's love story took on a new chapter as the years passed. They had weathered the storm and emerged more vital than ever.

Their children found motivation in this reconciliation. The family dynamic shifted, and a newfound sense of unity and respect blossomed. Through years of healing and personal growth, she found happiness and paved the way for a better future for her family. Her story became a testament to the power of forgiveness, resilience, and unwavering strength.

48

A Night of Passion and Desire: The Beginning of Forever

Donna and I were excited as we embarked on this new chapter of our lives together. She had found solace in a small apartment near her workplace in Quakertown at Classic Temps. The anticipation of our weekends together in my Philadelphia residence was almost too much to bear. On that first evening, as we gazed into each other's eyes, we made a promise to refrain from physical intimacy until her divorce was final. The air crackled with anticipation, but we knew the importance of patience and respect for the process.

But fate had other plans for us. In a mere hour, our resolve crumbled beneath our undeniable connection. The magnetic pull between us was irresistible, despite any restraint we had previously agreed upon. In a passionate frenzy, we shed our clothes like the burdens of the past, revealing the raw vulnerability of our naked bodies. As we intertwined, our lips met in a fervent kiss that spoke volumes of the desire coursing through our veins. Each touch and every caress ignited a fire within us, fueling an unbridled passion.

There was no room for inhibitions in our love, for we embraced our bodies and our desires with unabashed enthusiasm. The night enveloped us, its darkness serving as a canvas for the vivid strokes of passion we painted upon it. Time seemed irrelevant as we explored the depths of our connection, surrendering to the intoxicating allure of our shared desires. With Donna, I finally experienced reciprocated love, where her deep longing for me mirrored my own efforts. I basked in the overwhelming joy of Donna's desire at that precise moment. Her ardor and openness made me feel cherished and adored, as if I were the only person in the world capable of igniting such a flame within her. This feeling resonated deep within my soul, assuring me that our bond was strong and built on a foundation of passion, trust, and genuine affection. Little did I know that this night, where our bodies melded and our desires intertwined, would be the start of a lifelong journey. Donna, the embodiment of desire and strength, would later become my wife, and together, we would traverse the highs and lows of life with unwavering devotion.

Weekend Getaways: A Story of Love, Passion, and Adventure

From that first intimate night at my place in Philadelphia, the anticipation of our weekends together became an exhilarating ritual. As the week wore on, our hearts would beat in sync, eagerly awaiting Friday night, when Donna would arrive from Quakertown.

Our evening would always begin with happy hours at the vibrant Copabanana, nestled in the bustling South Street area. The ambiance of the vibrant establishment set the stage for our budding romance. We would indulge in their legendary juicy burgers with golden, greasy, irresistible fries. The pièce de resistance, however, was the jumbo-sized margaritas, each sip igniting our senses and elevating our spirits. We would clasp hands, our excitement palpable, as we toasted to the start of our weekend adventure.

With our hearts intertwined, we would stroll hand in hand, the city lights illuminating our path as we returned to my house. The anticipation in the air was electric. Slowly, we would undress each other, each button and zipper, revealing the vulnerability and desire that lay beneath our clothing. Our eyes locked, filled with passion and longing, as we surrendered to the intimate connection that bound us together. We shared moments filled with unbridled love, tenderness, and a profound sense of belonging in that sacred space.

Saturday mornings would greet us with a renewed sense of adventure. We would dance our way into the day, heading to the glamorous Monte Carlo Night Club, an enchanting haven of rhythm and movement on South Street. The music pulsated through our veins, guiding our bodies as we effortlessly intertwined on the dance floor. We found solace and freedom in each other's arms, losing ourselves in the night's euphoria.

We also immersed ourselves in the magic of the silver screen, losing ourselves in captivating movies that transported us to different worlds. Art galleries became our haven, where we marveled at the masterpieces that stirred our souls and sparked conversations that deepened our connection. At the theater we witnessed captivating performances that evoked laughter, tears, and a shared appreciation for the beauty of storytelling. And on sunny afternoons, we would bask in the serenity of Penn's Landing, enjoying leisurely picnics by the waterfront, savoring each bite, and relishing in the simplicity of our togetherness.

49

Donna Moves in and Oma's Misunderstanding

Donna and I were head over heels in love, cherishing our weekends together for two delightful years. But the desire to be in each other's arms every day grew more robust, and in 2004, we took the plunge. Donna bid farewell to her job in Quakertown and moved in with me in the vibrant city of Philadelphia.

Oma had been living with me on the first floor for the past eight years. Oma's doctor always claimed that she had an "old brain" but not dementia. Little did we know that this old brain would lead to some hilarious misunderstandings. As Donna and I settled into our cozy new lower-level apartment, Oma's excitement was palpable. However, her brain seemed to have concocted a whimsical twist. Because of our close bond and my attentive care, Oma had become convinced that I was her beloved husband!

When Donna moved in with us, Oma couldn't quite fathom why her "husband" brought another woman into her home. Donna and I found the situation utterly amusing. We couldn't help but chuckle at the comical nature of Oma's misconception. As the months went by, Donna and I cherished our time together, basking in the warmth of our new home. Oma's perception changed, and her interactions with Donna became more pleasant. Our lives became a delightful blend of love, laughter, and the occasional confusion caused by Oma's innocent mix-up. We embraced the situation's absurdity, finding joy in the most unexpected places.

Oma's Wild Birthday Adventure

In May 2004, Oma was about to turn ninety. She had her heart set on throwing a grand garden party and inviting all her dear friends from the German Society, from which she had retired eight years prior. Our city garden, which had won many accolades, was the perfect venue for this momentous occasion. Because we had more than fifty guests, we knew we had to go the extra mile to ensure it was memorable.

Oma surprised us with her unique birthday-gift request. Despite being legally hard of hearing and occasionally confusing, she remained a strong-willed German lady. So, imagine our astonishment when she declared that her ultimate birthday wish was to embark on a cross-country adventure in a motor home! It was as if she had unleashed her inner daredevil, ready to conquer the vast landscapes of the United States.

The garden party itself was a resounding success. We spared no effort in ensuring that the food was delicious, with a feast fit for royalty. An organ player and an accordion player filled the air with music, transporting us back to Oma's era.

But the highlight of the evening was the heartfelt speeches praising Oma's remarkable life journey. And, of course, we couldn't resist indulging in some good old-fashioned sing-alongs, belting out the cherished German songs that Oma held dear. As the night ended, we secretly hoped that Oma would wake up the next day and forget about her audacious desire to traverse the United States in a motor home. But alas, she woke up with an unwavering determination, ready to embark on her wild birthday adventure. With her spirit undeterred and her heart set on exploring the vast American landscapes,

Oma was a force to be reckoned with.

50

The Adventure Taking Shape: Embracing Adventure in the Rialta VW

Since we couldn't convince my spirited nonagenarian mother to give up her dream of celebrating her birthday by traversing the vast expanse of the United States, we embraced the idea and turned it into an unforgettable adventure for all of us—Oma, Donna, and myself. Our journey began with two weeks of camping shows and RV dealerships, eagerly seeking the perfect motor home to accommodate the three of us on this epic escapade. We were determined to find a compact, fuel-efficient, and easy-to-drive vehicle that would become our home away from home. After exploring many RV showrooms and marveling at the options, we stumbled upon the Winnebago Rialta, a true masterpiece that seamlessly blended beauty, technology, and power into one sleek package. We were instantly captivated when our eyes met its unique design and aerodynamic lines.

This Class C motor home was a marvel, boasting all the creature comforts and conveniences we could dream of. Measuring a mere twenty-one feet, the Rialta proved incredibly fuel-efficient and maneuverable. But its compact size belied a surprising spaciousness and unparalleled comfort. The interior of the Rialta was a marvel. It featured a cozy double bed and a single bed, ensuring a good night's sleep for all of us. The shower and small bathroom provided a touch of luxury, while the cooking facility allowed us to whip up delicious meals on the go. And let's not forget the comfortable sitting area, perfectly accommodating the three of us for lively conversations and shared laughter. With our hearts set on the Rialta, we made it ours.

The anticipation and excitement were palpable as we signed the papers, knowing that this remarkable motor home would be our trusted companion on this grand adventure. And so, with the Rialta as our chariot, we were ready to hit the open road in style, embarking on the adventure of a lifetime. The possibilities were endless, and the thrill of the unknown beckoned us forward. From the majestic mountains to the serene coastlines, we were eager to explore every nook and cranny of this beautiful country.

51

Across the USA: Virginia

In the summer of 2004, Donna, Oma, and I—along with Oma's beloved bird, Beppe—embarked on a wild, hilarious escapade in our brand-spanking-new motor home. It was one heck of a ride!

Oma was determined to make this trip, wheelchair and all. I, at sixty-three, was ready to embrace the madness, and the free-spirited Donna eagerly joined the party. Our insatiable thirst for adventure and the excitement of making our dreams a reality fueled us. The Rialta, our trusty motor home, was equipped with the latest technology, and we had a laptop mounted between the passenger and driver seats. We loaded it with the first GPS map system on the market.

We were like high-tech pioneers, ready to conquer the great unknown! Whenever the GPS announced a turn through the car speaker, Oma would perk up and ask, "Where is this guy giving us directions?" We couldn't resist teasing her: We told Oma that a little guy was way up in the sky, perched on a satellite, watching our every move. And when it was time for us to make a turn, he would magically call us over the speaker and tell us which way to go. Oma's eyes widened with amazement! Every day of our trip, without fail, she would ask us, "Hey, is that guy still up in the sky watching us drive?" And, of course, we couldn't let her down. "Yes, Oma, he's still up there, monitoring us!" Oh, the joy on her face was priceless. She'd sit in the passenger seat, glancing up at the sky now and then to check if our imaginary satellite guy was still on duty.

Our first stop? Claytor Lake State Park in Virginia. This place was no ordinary park. It offered various recreational activities and boasted a breathtaking lake view that would leave you speechless. The natural surroundings were straight from a postcard– like stepping into a surreal wonderland.

Oma was quite the bird lover, despite her limited vision and hearing. She proudly carried her birdcage every morning in Philly, housing her two feathered friends, Chicco and Beppe, out into the yard for a delightful breakfast ritual. Unfortunately, this ritual would take a hilarious turn. One fateful morning, I joined Oma outside for breakfast, only to find she'd forgotten to bring out the birdcage. She asked me to fetch it, and I was in for a surprise! As I picked up the cage, I noticed a mummified bird lying on the bottom. It turned out that Chicco had silently passed away some time ago without Oma knowing. I exclaimed, "Oma, your bird is...well, let's just say he's no more!" She calmly replied, "Oh, I noticed he was reticent lately. That explains why."

Fast forward to our first campground at the picturesque Claytor Lake State Park in Virginia. I carefully set up the cage for Oma on the picnic table, and Beppe, being the curious bird she was, got all excited at the sight of those towering trees and the melodic orchestra of chirping birds around her. She wanted to join the nature party. Filled with inspiration, I quickly returned to the motor-home and grabbed scissors. I gently clipped Beppe's wings, ensuring she couldn't soar away. From then on, whenever we settled at a new campground, I'd place Beppe on a nearby tree branch. She seemed content, happily watching us from her arboreal perch. It was like she had her own VIP seat for our adventures.

But as we were preparing to leave a campground one day, Oma brought the birdcage inside, and Donna settled in next to me while I took the wheel. About thirty minutes into our drive, Oma's voice broke the silence: "Beppe is silent. Is she okay?" Donna turned around, glanced at the cage, and exclaimed, "Beppe is not in the cage!" In that heart-stopping moment, it hit me like a ton of feathers: We had accidentally left Beppe perched on a tree branch at our previous campground. We made a swift U-turn and raced back, the anticipation building with every passing minute. And what do you know? An hour later, as we arrived at the scene, there she was—Beppe, still sitting on the branch, welcoming us with enthusiastic squawks, as if to say, "What took you so long?" From that day on, we never forgot to double-check that Beppe was safe in our care before hitting the road.

This was also the first time Oma had stayed at a campground, so we played a little prank on her. Far from civilization, deep in the wilderness, we informed her that survival was becoming more and more difficult. We spun a tale of feasting on roadkill, snakes, and wild creatures. We even declared that our pizza feast that evening would be our last taste of civilization. In her unique way, Oma switched gears and spoke solely in German. Maybe she tried to annoy Donna into joining the adventure, or perhaps she still thought I was her long-lost husband. Either way, the language barrier added another layer of comedy to our already-outrageous journey.

We spent a few glorious days at Claytor Lake State Park, indulging in various outdoor activities. And guess what? Oma even went fishing in her wheelchair! The sight of her rolling up to the water's edge, ready to reel in the day's catch, was a sight to behold. We couldn't help but laugh and cheer her on as she embraced the thrill of the hunt, wheelchair and all. Our next destination was the music mecca itself: Nashville, Tennessee.

52

Across the USA: Tennessee

Frogs, Cowboys, and Dancing Delights: A Wild Birthday Adventure

After arriving at the campground, we headed straight for the shower to freshen up, where we were greeted by an unusual sight: a shower pan filled with tiny frogs! Those little amphibians had found their way into the warm shower and enjoyed the cozy water just as much as we did. They were everywhere, hopping around, seemingly having the time of their lives. It was like a miniature frog party had taken over the bathroom! Undeterred by this frog frolicking, we quickly freshened up and headed to the renowned Wild Horse Saloon, where country music dreams come true.

The Wild Horse is a cowboy's paradise on steroids: a Wild West–themed extravaganza where the horses have traded their saddles for dance shoes and the cowboys have mastered the art of line dancing better than John Travolta in his prime. As you step inside, the atmosphere hits you like a bolt of lightning—but instead of electricity, it's infused with the electrifying energy of country music. The walls are adorned with vintage cowboy hats and neon signs that scream *yeehaw!* The smell of fried chicken and barbecue wafts through the air, tempting your taste buds to dive into Southern indulgence.

The Wild Horse Saloon is not just your average honky-tonk joint; it's a full-blown entertainment extravaganza. There's a massive stage where talented musicians from all over the country gather to strum their guitars and belt out songs about lost loves, pickup trucks, and dogs named Hank. The acoustics are so good that even if a rooster tried to crow, he'd sound like a young Dolly Parton.

But the music is just the beginning of the Wild Horse experience. This place has a dance floor that can accommodate more boot-scooting moves than you can count. Including two-stepping to "Cotton-Eyed Joe," you'll witness the most impressive choreography east of the Mississippi. It's like a real-life version of *Dancing with the Stars*, except you've got regular folks who can spin and twirl like tornadoes instead of celebrities. And if you're feeling a little rusty in the dance department, fear not! The Wild Horse Saloon has you covered, offering dance lessons for those who want to impress their friends with fancy footwork. So, even if you've got the coordination of a newborn giraffe, they'll have you swinging and swaying like a true country connoisseur in no time.

Now, let's talk about the drinks. The Wild Horse Saloon has a bar that stretches longer than a Texas highway and features all the classics, from ice-cold beer to smooth whiskey. And if you fancy something a little more adventurous, they'll whip up a cocktail that'll make you holler louder than a rodeo cowboy.

We settled in, ready to have a great time. But the real showstopper was my dear Oma, who, at ninety years old and legally blind, couldn't contain her excitement about hitting the dance floor. With a mischievous grin, I guided her onto the dance floor. As the music started playing, I began circling Oma, showing off my "sexy" dance moves—or at least attempting to! Donna couldn't help but burst into laughter as she watched us. Oma, feeling the energy of the music and my enthusiastic moves, was beaming with joy. In her mind, she was the dancing queen, and I was her loyal dance partner, making her feel like she was leading the way. We twirled, shuffled, and laughed together, creating a spectacle that brought smiles to everyone's faces. I couldn't wipe the grin off my face, knowing that I had made my dear Oma's night truly unforgettable.

The next day, we were off to the Grand Ole Opry House, a place that's seen more rhinestones and cowboy boots than a cattle ranch on prom night. This iconic venue is the shining star of country music, where legends have swung their heartstrings and left audiences hootin' and hollerin'. It's a splendid entertainment palace, where the walls are adorned with sequins and the air is thick with the smell of fried chicken and sweet Tennessee whiskey. As you step inside, you're greeted by the ghostly whispers of Hank Williams and Dolly Parton, who've left their musical mojo embedded in every corner.

The stage is a masterpiece, carved from the finest oak and sprinkled with the tears of aspiring musicians dreaming of making it big. It's witnessed more guitar solos than a rock 'n' roll convention, and the sound system is so powerful it can make your mama's biscuits rise from twenty miles away. The audience comes from far and wide, decked out in their finest plaid shirts and cowboy hats, ready to stomp their boots and holler like a pack of wild coyotes. It's a sight to behold, watching these folks let loose their inner country star.

And let's not ignore the backstage area, where the air is thick with superstition and the echoes of nervous performers. Legend says that if you stand in front of the mirror and sing "Jolene" three times, Dolly Parton herself will appear, granting you the power to tease your hair to unprecedented heights. The Grand Old Opry House is a shrine to all things twangy and toe-tapping, where dreams are born and legends are made. After a few days in Nashville, our next destination was the one and only Memphis, Tennessee, a place where the rhythm of the blues flows through the streets like a never-ending river.

Memorable Mayhem in Graceland

Memphis is practically synonymous with Elvis, and you can't flick a guitar pick without hitting a tribute artist or a souvenir shop dedicated to the hip-shaking legend. We parked our motor home in a quirky RV park outside the city. The owner, a self-proclaimed Elvis impersonator, greeted us with a voice so deep and gravelly that I swore it could shake the very foundations of Graceland.

With our trusty map in hand (which was probably printed in the prehistoric era), we set off to explore the city. Our first stop was Beale Street, where the soulful sounds of blues music seemed to seep out of every pore. Oma, with her nearly nonexistent eyesight, had a unique way of experiencing the music: She would tap her feet and sway her body in rhythm while sitting in a wheelchair several feet from the street musician.

As we entered the visitor center at Graceland for our first encounter with the staff, a group of Elvis impersonators welcomed us, each more bejeweled and hip-shaking than the last. They sang, danced, and offered to sign autographs, making us feel like we had entered some alternate universe where Elvis clones were running amok. Once we managed to tear ourselves away from them, we embarked on the mansion tour. As we strolled through the opulent rooms adorned with gold records and extravagant decor, I couldn't help but imagine what living like the King himself would have been like. But the highlight of our Graceland escapade was undoubtedly the Elvis-themed souvenir shop, with Elvis-themed trinkets and memorabilia covering every inch of shelf space.

As we bid farewell to Graceland, we couldn't help but reflect on the absurdity and joy accompanying our visit. Our time at Graceland was filled with laughter and a healthy dose of Elvis mania. It was an experience we couldn't forget and a tale we would regale friends and family with for years.

Next Stop: The Memphis Zoo!

We strolled into the zoo, feeling like a bunch of explorers on a safari. First up was the lion enclosure. Those majestic creatures can roar like nobody's business! But guess what? The lions must have sensed my unease, because they started a synchronized dance routine instead of roaring. I'm telling you, it was like a feline version of *Dancing with the Stars.* I couldn't stop laughing.

Next up, we ventured into the gorilla habitat. These primates had a sense of humor that could rival that of a stand-up comedian. One gorilla, let's call him Bob, decided it was time to show off his impression skills. He mimicked every zoo visitor, from their walk to their facial expressions, with such precision that we were all in stitches.

But the real showstopper of the day was the penguin exhibit—these tuxedo-wearing birds were the life of the party! They shuffled around with such swagger, as if they were auditioning for a Las Vegas revue. And when one penguin slipped on a patch of ice, causing a chain reaction of slipping and sliding, it was a slapstick masterpiece.

House of Piggly Wiggly

During our time in Memphis, the buzz about this mysterious house reached our ears. The locals whispered tales of its eccentricities: a vibrant pink exterior adorned with neon lights and a massive sign.

Naturally, our curiosity piqued, and we knew we couldn't leave the city without seeing this residence. With a mix of excitement and skepticism, we set out to find the infamous house. We followed the directions the locals gave, who had a twinkle in their eyes as they spoke of the wacky wonders that awaited us. And there it was, standing tall and proud, like a beacon of whimsy in an ordinary neighborhood. The House of Piggly Wiggly was a sight to behold. Its pink facade practically glowed in the daylight, and the neon lights around the entire structure illuminated the surrounding area, ensuring it couldn't be missed. We marveled at the giant sign that loomed above the entrance, announcing its name with a flourish.

But here's the catch: We never ventured inside. The owner had transformed his home into a private museum with peculiar artifacts and oddities. Sadly, the museum was not open to the public, leaving us and many others to fantasize about the wonders beyond those pink walls. We stood outside, noses pressed against the iron gate, our imaginations running wild with visions of secret passageways, talking paintings, and a treasure trove of bizarre collectibles. Oh, how we longed to step inside and witness the magic that awaited us. Alas, it was not meant to be. It symbolized the unexpected, showcasing the creativity and eccentricity of the most unlikely places. It reminded us to embrace life's quirky side and never be afraid to let our imaginations run wild.

53

Across the USA: Louisiana

As we bid farewell to Memphis, our trusty motor home carried us to the vibrant city of New Orleans, where we embarked on an unforgettable journey of sights, sounds, and surprises.

Our first stop was the iconic Jackson Square, a bustling hub of artistic expression and lively entertainment. We found ourselves drawn to the melodic tunes of a street performer, whose music reverberated through the square, captivating our souls. With the rhythm in our hearts, we entered the magnificent St. Louis Cathedral, where the hallowed halls whispered stories of faith and history.

Eager to embrace the city's mystique, we visited the Voodoo Museum, a peculiar yet fascinating place. With wide-eyed curiosity, we explored the mystical artifacts and learned about the intriguing world of voodoo. We purchased a voodoo doll to honor my dear Oma, hoping it would bring her good luck and ward off mischievous spirits. Speaking of voodoo, we couldn't resist delving deeper into the subject by reading up on the infamous Li Grande Zombi, a powerful and essential voodoo spirit. The tales surrounding this mystical figure sent shivers down our spines and piqued our curiosity to uncover more supernatural secrets.

Of course, a visit to New Orleans would only be complete with a tour down the infamous Bourbon Street. The tantalizing aromas guided us to the renowned Gumbo Shop restaurant. We greedily ordered their signature blackened fish and a steaming bowl of gumbo soup for each of us. Alas, fate had a tricky hand to play, for the rich flavors left poor Oma feeling a tad under the weather. Donna hurried Oma to the restroom, only to encounter an unfortunate mishap herself. Let's say Oma's upset stomach unexpectedly affected Donna's dress, leaving us all in stitches (and not the good kind!). We had to rush back to the motor home to tend to Oma's needs and help Donna freshen up, dashing our hopes of embarking on a thrilling ghost and vampire tour.

Undeterred by our misadventures, we made the most of our last day. Our destination was the enchanting home of the famed author Anne Rice. But to our dismay, we discovered that someone had locked the gates of her house and adorned them with a FOR SALE sign. Undeterred, we gazed upon the exterior's grandeur, imagining the captivating tales that might have unfolded within those walls.

Unexpected twists and turns filled our time in New Orleans. From toe-tapping melodies in Jackson Square to the mishaps at the Gumbo Shop restaurant and the elusive Anne Rice's house, we embraced the chaos and laughter accompanying our adventures. New Orleans left an indelible mark on our hearts and memories with its rich history and vibrant energy.

54

Across the USA: Texas

Mustang Island State Park: Tacos, Tequila, and a Wild Mustang Island Fiesta

As we drove into the park, the salty breeze filled the air, instantly invigorating our spirits. The park sprawled across 3,954 acres, with miles of pristine shoreline just waiting to be explored. We parked our motor home on the beach, excited to immerse ourselves in the wonders of Mustang Island.

Our first day was all about relaxation and soaking up the sun. We set up our beach chairs, slathered on sunscreen, and marveled at the vastness of the Gulf of Mexico before us. My mother, an adventurous soul, decided to dip in the ocean. She may have been ninety, but her spirit remained as youthful as ever. We laughed and cheered her on as she fearlessly waded into the water, creating a delightful memory that still brings a smile to our faces.

We had initially planned to leave before the weekend, but when we heard about the upcoming festivities, we couldn't resist staying one more day. And boy, what a decision that turned out to be! We were warned that the beach would be packed with motor homes, trucks, and campers, all gearing up for a massive beach cookout. Even the birds seemed to have insider information, flocking in anticipation of the feast that awaited them. It was like they had their secret society ready to dive into the discarded fish lining the beach. Talk about a party of winged foodies! But the real highlight of our extended stay was when we crossed paths with two wild and adventurous characters, Flash and Toni. These guys were a sight to behold, with bandannas wrapped around their heads and a zest for life that was simply infectious. In no time, we found ourselves fast friends, laughing and living life to the fullest. Oma wasted no time joining the party. She was a force to be reckoned with, ready to embrace every moment like a party animal.

Now, here's where things got even funnier. I had a secret stash of Jägermeister hidden away in our motor home, and I decided it was the perfect time to break it out and share the fun with our new friends. You should have seen their faces when I unveiled that big bottle! As the evening unfolded, Flash took charge of the grill mounted on the back of his truck. This guy was a grill-master extraordinaire and wasted no time whipping up some mouthwatering California fish tacos.

But it wasn't just the tacos that stole the show; Flash's homemade salsa added a zing of flavor to every bite. In her triumphant state, Oma couldn't help but beam with delight as if she had found true love in every taco. Flash would playfully tease Oma with his charismatic smile, saying, "It's all good, Oma!" And Oma, with a mischievous twinkle in her eye, would play along, pretending like she was making out with Flash, much to everyone's amusement. It was like a hilarious novella unfolding right before our eyes.

But the laughter didn't stop there. Oma told our new friends she was celebrating her ninetieth birthday, and let me tell you, that turned the party up to eleven! Suddenly, the energy skyrocketed, and the festivities took on a new level of excitement. Nearby strangers joined in the merriment, raising their glasses and toasting Oma's incredible milestone. We all indulged in the delectable homemade tacos, savoring each flavorful bite while sharing stories and laughter. The combination of Flash's culinary skills, Oma's infectious joy, and the camaraderie we had formed with our newfound friends made for a truly unforgettable evening. It was a wild, hilarious, and heartwarming experience that will forever be etched in our memories. The next day, with a tinge of sadness but hearts full of laughter, we bid farewell to Mustang Island and set our sights on the next adventure in Galveston's historic district.

Oma's Voodoo Doll Adventure: A Side-Splitting Quest for Good Luck

In Galveston, Oma decided to bring some good luck into our lives with the voodoo doll we'd purchased at the Voodoo Museum during our stop in New Orleans, hoping it would ward off mischievous spirits and bring some good fortune.

First, we needed a piece of hair from Oma to personalize the doll, which Donna snipped from Oma's head. We carefully wrapped it around the doll's neck, creating a connection between Oma and her mystical companion. That doll was a sight to behold! It had a black wire-shaped head, a white mask, and a fabulous green dress with a rainbow-colored hip band. And to top it all off, sticks protruded from its arms and legs, emphasizing its extremities.

Next came the critical task of writing a wish for the doll. Oma, who was nearly blind and struggled to sign her name, suddenly became a wordsmith when it came to asking for money, writing a whopping five lines! Oma wanted to win substantial money to treat Donna and me to a lavish dinner. She dreamed of having so much money that she could hop from one restaurant to another without a care in the world.

Now, here's where things took a hilarious turn. As Oma prepared to activate the spell by inserting a needle into the doll, Donna couldn't help but make a cheeky comment. She joked that if Oma had that much money, we'd have to bring a portable toilet so Oma could relieve herself at the restaurant table! You see, during our last dinner outing, poor Oma couldn't hold her food in any longer and vomited all over Donna when they rushed to the bathroom. Oh, the memories!

With the wish written, the needle inserted, and Oma beaming excitedly, we had to find a quiet place to store the doll. I suggested the motor-home bathroom, but Donna quickly shot that idea down, mentioning that her butt was always in there. So, after much deliberation, we decided to tuck the doll under the seat bench, hoping it would work its magic from there. Oma's face was lit up with hope and anticipation, dreaming of all the money we would have by the time we reached Las Vegas in a few days. We laughed and joked, imagining a future filled with extravagant dinners and carefree restaurant-hopping. Little did we know that Oma's voodoo-doll adventure would bring us laughter and a sense of togetherness and joy that money couldn't buy.

And so, with Oma's wish sealed within the doll and our hearts filled with laughter, we continued our journey, eagerly awaiting the surprises that awaited us along the way. Maybe the doll would work its magic and bring us more than just financial fortune. Perhaps it would bring us unforgettable moments and cherished memories that would last a lifetime. Our motor home took us to Galveston's historic district the next day.

A Whimsical Escapade: Galveston's Historic District and the Fantastical Voyage

History and imagination intertwine most delightfully in Galveston's historic district. Picture this: the sun shining, a salty breeze filling the air, and our hearts filled with adventure. As we strolled through the charming streets, we couldn't help but be captivated by the vibrant energy that permeated the district. Quaint Victorian-style buildings stood tall, colorful facades telling stories of a bygone era. It was as if we had stepped into a whimsical world where time had taken a delightful pause.

One sight caught our attention: a majestic harbor with a cruise ship named *Elation* docked at its side. As we watched passengers board the boat, a naughty thought crossed our minds. What if we could magically transport ourselves onto that ship and embark on a grand adventure? In our playful imaginations, we envisioned ourselves as part of the lively crowd, eagerly awaiting the voyage ahead. We conjured up images of waving goodbye to the onlookers, feeling the excitement build as the ship set sail.

Now, let's add a touch of embellishment to this tale, shall we? As we daydreamed about being aboard the *Elation*, a whimsical character named Captain Quirksalot appeared out of thin air. With a twinkle in his eye and a mischievous grin, he offered us a magical ticket that would grant us passage onto the ship. How could we resist such an enchanting offer? We boarded the ship with a sense of wonder and anticipation. Little did we know that this fantastical voyage would take us to the most extraordinary places.

As the ship sailed from the harbor, we found ourselves in a world of pure imagination. We visited mythical lands where unicorns roamed freely and mermaids sang enchanting melodies. We danced with pirates, who were exceptionally friendly and explored hidden-treasure-filled caves. The ship seemed to have a personality, with secret passageways leading to whimsical rooms filled with laughter and merriment.

But alas, all good things must come to an end. As the *Elation* made its way back to Galveston, we bid farewell to our newfound friends and stepped back onto solid ground. Our hearts were filled with joy and a renewed sense of adventure.

I must confess that this tale is a whimsical blend of reality and imagination. While we didn't board the *Elation* that day, our journey through Galveston's historic district was a delightful adventure in its own right. We may not have sailed the seas, but we did sail through the pages of history, exploring the stories that echoed through the charming streets and vibrant buildings. So, if you ever find yourself in Galveston, let your imagination run wild. Who knows what fantastical tales await you? Whether watching cruise ships from afar or embarking on a whimsical journey in your mind, let the spirit of adventure guide you as you create your own magical story in this enchanting corner of the world.

Tropical Paradise: Exploring the Enchanting Moody Gardens

The next day, we ventured into the enchanting world of Moody Gardens in Galveston. Our anticipation grew as we approached the pyramid-shaped tropical gardens, for we knew we were about to embark on a journey into a realm of vibrant beauty and exotic wonders.

As we entered, it was as if we had entered a different world altogether. The air was thick with the sweet scent of tropical flowers, and the lush greenery surrounded us, creating a serene and magical atmosphere. It felt like we had been transported to a faraway paradise featuring a breathtaking array of tropical plants and flowers in every shade and hue imaginable. The vibrant colors danced before our eyes as if nature was putting on a show just for us. We marveled at the intricate designs and delicate petals, entirely captivated by the sheer beauty surrounding us.

And the birds! Strange and exotic creatures fluttered about, their vibrant feathers adding more wonder to the already-mesmerizing scene. We couldn't help but feel a sense of awe as we watched them gracefully soar through the air, their melodic songs filling the atmosphere with joy. As we ventured further, we noticed that the beauty of Moody Gardens extended beyond its tropical oasis. The surrounding area was equally stunning, with palm trees lining the streets, swaying gently in the warm breeze. The sight of these majestic trees evoked a sense of tranquility and relaxation, as if time had slowed down to match the peaceful rhythm of the island.

Nets, Nostalgia, and New Beginnings: A Day in Palacios

Next up was the quaint fishing village of Palacios, where the sunsets paint the sky in shades of red, and the harbor is filled with a vibrant display of colorful fishing boats. It was a day filled with wonder and nostalgia as we parked our motor home beside the fishing boats. We were enamored with the scene before us as the sun set and brightened the horizon. The harbor was lined with various fishing boats, each adorned with a unique charm. The boats stood proudly, their colorful hulls reflecting the last rays of sunlight, creating a picturesque scene that seemed straight out of a painting. What caught our attention were the green fishing nets hoisted up on cranes, adding an extra touch of character to the charming boats. Some vessels were weathered and worn, bearing the marks of countless fishing adventures. Yet, this nostalgia added to their allure, reminding us of their rich history and stories.

The names adorning each boat—*Mrs. Mina, Thunder II, Joshe & Jake, Vincent II, Lizzi I, Captain Bubba, Little Ernie, Santa Maria*—evoked a sense of curiosity and wonder. We imagined the tales behind each name, the adventures that had unfolded on the open sea. In the middle of the bustling scene, we saw an old fisherman sitting on the floor, his weathered hands carefully mending broken fishing nets, his skill evident in every precise movement. By his side stood an old dog, a loyal companion who seemed to share the fisherman's wisdom and experience. We watched in awe as the dedication and artistry were displayed before us. It was a reminder that even in today's technologically advanced world, some carry on age-old traditions, preserving the essence of their craft. The fisherman and his faithful canine companion were a testament to the resilience and beauty of their trade. As we watched him work, we admired his dedication and wondered about the stories that must have unfolded throughout his years at sea.

At that moment, we realized that Palacios was not just a fishing village, it was a place where time stood still, where the echoes of the past intertwined with the present. It was a place where the vivid colors of the boats mirrored the vibrant spirits of the fishermen who sailed them. Leaving the fisherman to his craft, we continued our stroll along the harbor, taking in the sights and sounds of this charming village. The evening sky painted a breathtaking backdrop, as if nature itself were applauding the town's beauty.

A Wild Bike Ride and a Daring Stage Show

Donna and I embarked on a thrilling bike ride to explore the area around us the next day. Little did we know that this adventure would take a hilarious and unexpected turn. As we pedaled, we stumbled upon an abandoned open-air theater with a giant sign that read, DO NOT ENTER.

Well, you know us; we couldn't resist the allure of forbidden places. Ignoring the sign, we hopped off our bikes and boldly crossed the barricade to enter the theater. Wow, what a sight it was! The stage was massive, and the stadium seating looked like it hadn't seen an audience in ages. The sides of the theater were overgrown with tall grass and weeds, giving it an eerie yet enchanting vibe. Donna decided to sit in the second row, while I, feeling inspired, couldn't resist the temptation of the stage. I started humming a catchy tune and tap dancing, Donna, applauding.

And that's when she threw down the ultimate challenge, daring me to dance naked on the stage. Now, I'm not one to back down from a dare, especially when it promises a lot of fun. Without wasting a moment, I sharpened my dance moves and seamlessly transitioned from tap dancing to seriously sexy moves. Slowly but surely, I began shedding my clothes, tossing my shirt and pants into the seating area where Donna was excitedly watching. As I continued dancing, I could feel the sexiness coursing through my veins, and I decided to turn up the heat. With each seductive movement, I shed another layer until I was completely naked. Donna couldn't contain her wild applause, cheering me on as I let my inhibitions melt away. It was a liberating and exhilarating experience.

After I was done, I gracefully thanked my imaginary audience and hopped off the stage, collecting my clothes. Donna and I burst into laughter, reveling in the absurdity of the moment. Who knew a bike ride could lead to a daring and unforgettable stage show? And so, that impromptu performance became a cherished memory in the story of our lives, reminding us constantly to embrace spontaneity and find joy in the unexpected. After all, life is too short to take ourselves too seriously.

A Blissful Day at Guadalupe River State Park

During our journey to San Antonio, we embarked on a delightful adventure to the enchanting oasis of Guadalupe River State Park. An atmosphere of happiness and excitement greeted us as soon as we parked our motor home and stepped outside.

Guadalupe State Park is a captivating oasis in the heart of Texas, where nature's beauty unfolds in a mesmerizing display, offering a delightful escape from the bustling city life. We were awestruck by the breathtaking Guadalupe River. Its gentle flow meanders through a tapestry of towering cypress trees, creating a picturesque backdrop that seems straight out of a dream. The rhythmic whispers of the river tell tales of serenity and beckon you to explore its hidden treasures.

We strolled the park's scenic trails, where every twist and turn reveals a new marvel of nature. Cascading waterfalls glistened in the sunlight, as if nature was putting on a dazzling show just for us. Ancient limestone cliffs stood as silent guardians of the park, their majestic presence evoking a sense of awe.

The park's vibrant wildlife added a touch of enchantment to our journey. Playful deer gracefully roamed the forest while mischievous squirrels darted through the trees, creating a lively symphony of nature's harmonies. And diving into the refreshing embrace of the Guadalupe River washed away any cares. Without hesitation, we waded into the crystal-clear waters, feeling the coolness enveloping our bodies and washing away the weariness from our journey.

As we ventured further into the river, we couldn't help but notice the vibrant scene unfolding around us. People of all ages floated downstream, their laughter echoing through the air. Some chose the comfort of a tube or a raft, while others surrendered themselves to the gentle current, allowing their bodies to float freely. It was a spectacle of pure bliss and carefree enjoyment. Guadalupe State Park is a sanctuary where time stands still, and the wonders of the natural world take center stage. It invites you to rediscover life's simple pleasures, connect with nature, and create memories that will forever be etched in your heart. So come, escape to this haven of beauty and adventure, and let Guadalupe State Park weave its spell around you.

A Memorable Journey to Big Bend National Park

As we cruised down the road the next day, a vibrant sign welcomed us to the Rio Grande Valley. To our delight, the streets were adorned with charming old-fashioned windmills, spinning gracefully in the warm breeze. On either side, majestic stone mountains stood tall, casting their shadow over the landscape. It felt like we were the only souls on the road.

Nature's creatures were busy going about their day. Busy buzzards scoured the area, searching for their next meal. We quickly learned not to leave food unattended on the table, as the clever vultures would swoop down and snatch it away in the blink of an eye. Hawks soared above, their keen eyes scanning for prey. We encountered Javelina wild pigs, their presence commanding attention as they watched us with an intensity that seemed to say, "You're our next meal."

Mingling with such untamed wildlife was an exhilarating yet slightly nerve-wracking experience. But the magic of the moment was undeniable. As we explored, we came across some wild donkeys grazing leisurely without seeming to mind our presence. They seemed almost within arm's reach, allowing us to observe their gentle nature up close. And then, as if the universe wanted to surprise us further, a rare sight unfolded before our eyes: a white donkey gracefully passing by, a vision of pure elegance against the backdrop of the rugged terrain.

The mighty Rio Grande flowed nearby, its tranquil waters connecting us to Mexico and offering a glimpse of another world across the river. The landscape was adorned with breathtaking cacti, their vibrant hues painting a picture of resilience and beauty.

During our adventure, we stumbled upon a charming little souvenir shop. It boasted a quirky Statue of Liberty guarding its entrance. We found a treasure trove of unique items, from stunning jewelry to beautiful wind chimes, soulful drums, mystical walking sticks, and even intriguing skulls. Each item held a story, a piece of the journey we were experiencing.

Our trip to Big Bend National Park was not just a mere excursion, it was a tapestry woven with vibrant colors and unforgettable moments. It was a testament to the wonders of nature and the joy of exploration.

55

Across the USA (and into Mexico!)

Our next stop was Zaragoza, a vibrant city in Mexico, where history meets modern charm and fills the air with infectious energy. The city's rich cultural heritage breathes life into every corner, from its magnificent architecture to its lively streets. Walking through its bustling plazas, you can feel the heartbeat of Zaragoza as it pulsates with passion and zest for life.

Exploring the winding streets, you discover hidden gems at every turn. Charming cafes invite you to savor the flavors of authentic Mexican cuisine, tantalizing my taste buds with delectable dishes like savory enchiladas and mouthwatering tacos. The aromas of freshly brewed coffee and warm churros filled the air, luring you into cozy patisseries where you indulged in sweet delights.

But beyond its cultural treasures, Zaragoza embraces modernity with open arms. Contemporary art galleries showcase the works of talented local artists, while trendy boutiques offer fashionable finds for every taste. And the city's parks and gardens provided an oasis of tranquility, inviting you to bask in the sunshine and soak in the beauty of nature. Zaragoza is a city that seamlessly blends the old with the new, the traditional with the innovative. It's where history whispers in your ear and the present swirls around you in a vibrant dance.

One day, we had decided to have some margaritas and indulge in authentic Mexican food. People warned us it might be best to leave our motor home on the American side and walk across the bridge—and they were right! We were pushing Oma in a wheelchair, navigating the bustling streets of Zaragoza. We couldn't help but feel a little on edge as we walked through the vibrant streets. After all, we were in a foreign land, and the unknown can always be a tad nerve-wracking.

We were on a mission for margaritas, and nothing would stop us! Finally, we stumbled upon a charming little restaurant. The aroma of spices and sizzling fajitas filled the air, instantly making our mouths water. We settled in, ordered our margaritas, and let the fiesta begin! As we sipped our refreshing drinks, laughter and joy abounded. Those margaritas packed quite the punch! The lively atmosphere and the tequila didn't take long to get the best of us. Our adventure in Zaragoza was an unforgettable experience. What started as a simple desire for margaritas turned into an extraordinary memory. We laughed and we indulged in the most delicious Mexican cuisine. And through it all, we felt safe and embraced by the warmth and hospitality of the Mexican people.

So, my friends, if you ever find yourself on an impromptu excursion to Zaragoza, leave your motor home behind. You never know what surprises await you, but one thing is sure: It will be a tale worth telling for years. Cheers to adventure, laughter, and unforgettable margaritas!

56

Across the USA: New Mexico

Albuquerque is a city steeped in history and culture, and we were determined to experience it all. We pulled up in our motor home in front of the legendary Aztec Motel on Route 66, and tiny houses stood proudly nearby, each adorned with various interesting artifacts. There were old car parts, rusty signs from days past, and even a vintage jukebox with timeless tunes. It was like stumbling upon an American treasure trove in the desert's heart. The motel itself was a sight to behold. In its heyday, it served as a popular stop for weary Route 66 travelers. We leisurely strolled around the motel grounds, immersing ourselves in the moment's magic. The artifacts around the neighboring houses grew more enchanting as the evening shadows danced upon them. Each piece had its own story, whispering tales of a bygone era.

Santa Fe Shenanigans: Art, Courts, and a Motor Home Adventure

We then set course for Santa Fe, nestled in the majestic Sangre de Cristo Mountains. As we rolled into downtown, the first thing that struck us was its unique blend of Spanish, Native American, and Western influences. The adobe buildings, adorned with vibrant turquoise doors and intricate ironwork, gave the entire area a charming and rustic feel. We explored the renowned Santa Fe Art Market. What a visual feast! Artists of all kinds showcased their masterpieces under colorful tents, filling every nook and cranny with paintings, sculptures, jewelry—you name it! My mother, in her wheelchair, couldn't resist conversing with one of the young artists, much to her delight and our amusement.

We then went to the city's supreme court building. You might think, "What's so exciting about a courthouse?" But being alone in the empty chamber with the majestic judge's bench and towering bookshelves was like stumbling upon a secret hideout in the legal world.

As much as we enjoyed exploring the art scene and the supreme court, it was time to indulge our taste buds. Santa Fe is famous for its mouthwatering cuisine, blending traditional New Mexican flavors with modern twists. We devoured green chili-infused dishes and sipped on prickly pear margaritas.

Lost in the Twilight: A Journey of Love and Loss

As the sun bid farewell to the diverse landscapes of Santa Fe on that fateful 4th of July in 2004, Oma, Donna, and I found ourselves immersed in bittersweet reflection. We reminisced about the vivid memories we had created during our cross-country trip across the USA—moments that had become the very essence of our journey. Every twist and turn had been an adventure, with joy and laughter echoing through our hearts. With heavy but excited hearts, we returned to our motor home, looking forward to what lay ahead on our next day of exploration. That evening, we sought the perfect vantage point to witness the Santa Fe fireworks—a spectacle illuminating the sky in splendid bursts of light.

As we marveled at the show, Donna's phone rang. The news broke us. Donna's ex-husband told us that Brandon, her precious twenty-five-year-old son, had gone riding on his beloved ATV and was now missing. Before the words could entirely escape his lips, a wave of instinctual grief washed over Donna. Deep down, she knew the unwavering truth: Brandon had collided with a large tree. The pain of loss churned within her—immeasurable and ceaseless.

In an instant, our cross-country odyssey transformed into a heart-wrenching journey of grief and reflection. Once paved with dreams and adventures, the road ahead felt dim and uncertain as I drove the motor home toward Albuquerque, all of us filled with unfathomable sorrow.

I embraced Donna tightly at the Albuquerque airport. She looked at me through tear-stained eyes, as if pleading for an answer to the unanswerable. Understanding the depths of her pain, I guided her toward the plane that would carry her back home, back to the reminders of a life forever altered.

With Donna's absence, the motor home became a silent vessel, filled with memories and echoes of broken hearts. We traversed the long stretches of highway that separated us from home, the journey now lacking the spark that had once fueled our wanderlust.

Throughout the years that followed, Donna carried a tremendous weight of grief. The pain of loss never entirely subsided, etching lines of sorrow onto her aged face. Despite her suffering, Donna found some comfort in the memories of our cross-country trip.

Despite cutting short our adventure, it still stands as a testament to the enduring power of love and resilience. Our bond, strengthened amid the beauty and tragedy of our journey, provided solace during the darkest days. As time passed, our travels became treasured stories, whispered in hushed tones through tears and laughter. I knew that Donna's spirit would endure, her love for Brandon forever etched within her heart.

57

The Decision to Tie the Knot

In 2007, after five incredible years of dating Donna, we found ourselves standing at the crossroads of our relationship, contemplating a decision that would forever change our lives: marriage.

It was a decision we never thought we would make when we first became friends. We had both agreed that marriage was not for us and that we would simply enjoy our time together. But as time passed, something shifted, and we felt a mutual desire to take that leap of faith. We had been filled with adventure and joy in the five years leading up to this moment. We embarked on countless journeys across the vast landscapes of the United States, exploring new places and creating memories that would last a lifetime. Our motor home became our home away from home as we embraced the freedom of the open road and the thrill of discovering new horizons together.

But it wasn't all carefree wanderlust. We also faced challenges head-on, supporting each other through thick and thin. We opened our hearts and our home to my aging mother, taking on the responsibility of caring for her with love and compassion. It was a testament to the strength of our bond and our commitment to family. And the pain of losing Brandon was unimaginable, testing our resilience and love for one another. Together, we navigated the depths of grief, finding solace in each other's arms and drawing strength from our shared memories of Brandon.

And so, as we stood at the precipice of matrimony, our hearts filled with a newfound understanding of the fragility and beauty of life, we realized that love was not just about the adventures and the laughter but also about weathering the storms together and supporting each other through the darkest times.

The excitement of planning our wedding at the Four Seasons Hotel in Philadelphia consumed us. The venue exuded an undeniable charm with its elegant architecture and impeccable service. It was the perfect backdrop to celebrate our love and commitment to one another. We wanted our wedding to be intimate, surrounded only by our closest loved ones. Our guest list included Donna and my mother, my daughter Sabine, her husband Jordan, Donna's mother, and her two boys, Brett and Kirk. It was a gathering of our cherished family, a merging of two worlds coming together in celebration.

The road to our wedding had its fair share of joys and challenges. We meticulously planned every detail, from the elegant floral arrangements to the delectable menu. Each decision was carefully made to create an atmosphere that embodied the essence of our love and the joy we felt in joining our lives together.

As the day approached, anticipation grew. We awoke the morning of our wedding in the opulent embrace of the Four Seasons with the promise of a lovely day ahead. The hotel became our sanctuary, where we could savor every moment, from the early-morning preparations to the late-night celebrations. Our wedding day was filled with laughter, tears, and heartfelt toasts. It was a day when love bloomed, and those who knew us best celebrated our union. The joy we felt radiated through every smile and embrace.

We faced joy and challenges in the early days of our marriage. We were determined to create a home that reflected our love and aspirations. Our living arrangements were unique, with us occupying the first and lower floors while the second and third floors were rented out to tenants. This allowed us to save money and invest it in renovating our living spaces.

We rolled up our sleeves and got to work, pouring our hearts into transforming our house into a sanctuary of love and comfort. Simplifying our lives became a priority as we recognized the importance of financial stability in building the future we envisioned. We reduced unnecessary expenses and redirected our resources toward the renovation project. It was a labor of love as we meticulously planned every detail, from the color palettes to the furniture arrangements, ensuring that our home truly reflected our unique style and shared vision.

One of the highlights of our home was the beautiful, award-winning Philadelphia city garden. We enlisted the help of a talented landscaper to transform it into a green oasis. With their expertise, our garden bloomed into a picturesque haven, complete with an enclosed wooden gazebo. We spent countless hours in this tranquil space, basking in the beauty of nature and cherishing the moments of serenity it provided. We even went the extra mile to make it a year-round retreat, installing heating in the pavilion for cozy winter evenings and air conditioning for refreshing summer escapes.

As the years passed, our home became a true reflection of our love and dedication. It became a sanctuary where we could retreat from the outside world, where our dreams took shape and our love grew. The garden symbolizes our commitment to creating a life filled with beauty and tranquility.

As the years passed, the blessings of both our beloved house at the Pocono Spring Estate and our Philadelphia home close to the well-known Italian Market enriched our lives. Both became the cornerstones of our existence, each offering a unique and fulfilling experience.

Our Philadelphia home provided us with the hustle and bustle of city life. We immersed ourselves in the rich culture and flavors of the neighborhood, indulging in delectable cuisine and exploring the hidden gems that lined the streets. It was where we could easily access all the amenities and excitement a city offers.

On the other hand, our Pocono home, located in the serene beauty of nature, offered a tranquil escape from the fast-paced city life. Recognizing the potential of this haven, we decided to turn it into an Airbnb, allowing us to generate income to cover the ever-increasing taxes and association fees while still using it when we wanted.

The Pocono Springs Estate, with its picturesque Crystal Lake, became our sanctuary for reconnecting with nature. We embarked on countless adventures, hiking through lush trails, casting our lines for fishing, and embracing the serenity of boating on the tranquil waters. It was a place where we could unwind and engage in recreational activities that brought us closer to the beauty of the natural world.

My mother had been living with us for many years, and it was a bittersweet journey of caring for her. Her presence brought depth and love to our lives as we navigated the joys and challenges of being caregivers. Oma was a remarkable woman, full of wisdom and grace. Her radiant smile could light up a room, and her warm embrace could heal even the deepest wounds. As she aged, it became clear that she needed our support and care.

Our top priorities were adjusting our routines and ensuring her comfort and well-being. From assisting with daily tasks to providing emotional support, we embraced our caregiver roles with unwavering dedication. Despite the responsibilities, we created countless memories together. We spent evenings gathered around the dining table, sharing stories and laughter over home-cooked meals. Oma would regale us with tales from her youth, transporting us to a bygone era filled with love, resilience, and the pursuit of dreams.

But as the years passed, her health began to decline. We faced the inevitable reality that we would have to say goodbye to this extraordinary woman who had shaped our lives in immeasurable ways. Her passing at ninety-six left an indelible mark on our hearts. The impact of Oma's loss reverberated through our lives. We mourned the physical absence of her warm embrace and the gentle sound of her laughter. In honoring her legacy, we celebrated the strength of our bond and the love that continues to connect us, even in her physical absence. We carry her spirit within us, a constant reminder of the power of love and the importance of cherishing those we hold dear.

Before I close this chapter, I want to emphasize the profound importance of caring for our loved ones until the end of their lives, especially when their health begins to fail. It is an incredibly challenging journey that demands immense physical, emotional, and mental strength. Yet, committing to be there for our loved ones until their last breath is a testament to the depth of our compassion and the power of human connection.

Taking on the role of a caregiver takes work. It requires sacrifices, sleepless nights, and a constant balancing act of responsibilities. There are moments of frustration, exhaustion, and doubt. But there is also an undeniable sense of fulfillment that comes from knowing we have done everything in our power to provide comfort and care to those who have nurtured us.

In today's fast-paced world, relying on nursing homes or assisted living facilities to care for our aging loved ones has become all too common. While these institutions can provide necessary medical care, they often lack the personal touch and individualized attention that comes from being cared for by family. When I was growing up, there was no question about it—you took care of your family members, no matter what.

Choosing to care for our loved ones until the end is a choice rooted in love, respect, and a deep understanding of the value of human connection. It is a choice that allows us to create lasting memories, share meaningful conversations, and provide comfort in the most vulnerable moments. It enables us to honor the bond that has shaped our lives and to give back to those who have given us so much.

58

Shadows and Strength: Navigating Life with Donna

Over the next ten years, even as Donna and I were creating cherished moments, we experienced some tough times. Donna's depression, which she'd battled since her younger years, reared its head again, exacerbated by the heart-wrenching loss of Brandon. Anguish left her grappling with the weight of unimaginable grief. Faced with such overwhelming darkness, Donna sought extensive treatment and counseling, desperately seeking a lifeline to guide her through the labyrinthine corridors of her desolation.

To aid in her quest for solace, Donna's healthcare providers prescribed an intricate assortment of medications, each intended to assuage the symptoms that plagued her and restore a semblance of equilibrium to her fragile psyche. But with them came side effects. A ceaseless cycle of weariness trapped Donna, the weight of which pressed upon her, compelling her to seek solace in sleep, sometimes to an excess that bordered on escape.

Donna now has trouble experiencing joys and passions that once ignited her spirit. And if the weight of her emotional turmoil was not enough, the medications added physical weight to her frame, an unwelcome reminder of the battles fought within. Yet, through it all, her depression remained, an unyielding shadow that cast its pall over her every waking moment. The indomitable spirit that had once burned brightly within her now flickered with uncertainty as she grappled with whether the darkness would recede.

As her partner and confidant, I stood by Donna's side, a steadfast beacon in her stormy sea. I witnessed her emotions ebb and flow, the anguish etched upon her face, and the silent battles fought within her. I yearned to understand the depths of her despair and the weight she carried on her weary shoulders. In my quest for empathy and understanding, I sought to peel back the layers of her experience to immerse myself in the tumultuous sea of emotions that Donna navigated daily. I wanted to walk a mile in her shoes, feel her burden's weight, and glimpse the world through her eyes. Only then could I hope to offer the solace and support she desperately needed.

Donna's ongoing struggle cast its shadow not only upon her but also upon the landscape of our shared existence and the emotions and challenges I faced as I stood by her side. Yet, despite the challenges we faced, I refused to let despair consume me. I drew strength from our love and the moments of joy and connection that still found their way into our lives. The responsibility weighed heavily on my shoulders as I grappled with the delicate balance of supporting Donna while also tending to my needs. There were moments of frustration and exhaustion when I questioned my capacity to be the pillar of strength she needed. Yet, in those moments, I reminded myself of the enduring love that bound us together, and I found the resilience to continue. I also recognized the importance of self-care. I committed to carving out time for activities that rejuvenated my spirit, allowing me to replenish my emotional reserves. I found solace in nature, taking leisurely walks, breathing fresh air, and finding solace in the world's beauty.

This chapter is a testament to the complexities of love and the strength required to navigate life while someone is battling depression. It is a reminder that the journey is not linear but a series of peaks and valleys, where both partners must find solace and understanding in each other's embrace.

59

Karla's Journey: A Heartwarming Adventure from Florida to Philly

There's something extraordinary about my sister, Karla, who has her own unique brand of spirituality. She didn't believe in God, yet she was all about the power of Saint Germain, the Earthkeeper. According to Karla, Saint Germain wasn't just some ordinary earthly being—he was from another planet!

Karla also believed that she was a Light-Worker. She claimed this special connection with Saint Germain and even had a spiritual name: Violet-Flame. I mean, talk about a name that makes you do a double-take. It's like she was trying to be a superhero or something! Every night, Karla would faithfully join a conference call with fellow self-proclaimed "light workers." They would listen to the head of the light workers, who supposedly had a direct line to communicate with Saint Germain himself. Can you imagine that conference call? I bet it was like a mix of a ritual and a motivational speech. But here's the kicker, my friends: You know that saying, "There ain't no such thing as a free lunch"? Well, there isn't a direct line to Saint Germain without a fee involved. Yep, Karla had to pay to be a part of this exclusive spiritual club. I can't imagine how much money she spent on those conference calls.

I don't want you to think I'm mocking my sister here. Honestly, I thought the whole thing was hilarious. I mean, who am I to judge? We all have our quirks. Karla's belief in Saint Germain and her light-worker status were quirky. But hey, if it made her happy and gave her some purpose in life, who was I to rain on her parade?

Karla also had a knack for leaving her mark everywhere she went. She had this bizarre habit of drawing hearts in the sand everywhere she stepped foot, which people found perplexing. She told me it was her unique way of spreading love. Who needs Cupid's arrow when you have Karla's sandy hearts, right?

But here's the kicker: She always had a challenging time spreading *actual* love. Karla was like a human roller coaster. One minute, she'd be all sweetness and light; the next, she'd unleash her inner volcano and erupt with rage. The truth was that my sister didn't care for most people. But animals were a different story! Karla had a heart as soft as a marshmallow for our furry friends, showering them with compassion and affection.

Karla was also the ultimate rebel, always living life on her terms. Who needs to follow those boring laws and signs, right? One sunny day, we found ourselves at the beach, where a big sign clearly stated, NO DOGS ALLOWED Did that stop Karla? Of course not! She strolled right by with her faithful pup, Penny, in tow, ignoring the disapproving glances from passersby. She had this mischievous twinkle in her eye, like she was saying, *Watch me break the rules, suckers!*

And if she ever needed flowers, forget going to the store. Nope, Karla would wake up at the crack of dawn, march over to any garden in the neighborhood, and snatch those beautiful blooms like she owned the place. It was like her own personal sunrise flower shop.

She also had a knack for turning any supermarket into her buffet. She'd stroll down the aisles, grabbing a bite here, a nibble there, without a care. She could've given the Cookie Monster a run for his money. But she saved her most audacious act of rebellion for our dinners with friends. She'd lean over, her eyes gleaming excitedly, and say, "Oh, let me taste that!" It didn't matter if it was a fancy steak or a humble plate of spaghetti—she wanted a piece of the action. And let me tell you, it always led to some hilarious reactions from our friends. They'd look at her like, *Karla, seriously, get your own meal!*

Karla's disregard for rules didn't always go unnoticed. One fateful day, a police officer caught her red-handed, walking her dog on that forbidden beach. He wagged his finger and warned her, "This is my third warning, young lady. Next time, you're going straight to the judge." Did she learn her lesson? No. The judge slapped her with a fine of $150, but it didn't phase her. She still took her dog back to that beach like a true rebel.

But Karla had her heartwarming moments, too. One took place on a beautiful day in March 2019 when I received a life-altering phone call. Karla, at 81, reached out to me from her cozy home in Lauderdale-by-the-Sea, Florida. She sounded unwell and expressed her desire to live with me and Donna at our house in Philly. I couldn't contain my joy at her request. Karla and I had always shared a special bond; having her with us made me smile. Donna and I packed our bags without hesitation and took a road trip to Florida to get her.

Arriving at Karla's tranquil haven, I felt a surge of excitement. She had always held a special place in her heart for her little brother, and now it was my turn to be there for her. Karla welcomed us with open arms, accompanied by her faithful companion, Penny. With her free-spirited nature, Karla insisted on leaving all her belongings behind. "Nothing matters more than Penny," she said, reminding me of her unwavering love for her furry friend. So, with Penny comfortably settled in the car, we hit the open road, ready to begin this new chapter together.

Upon reaching Philly, Karla's eyes sparkled with delight as she beheld the beautiful apartment that awaited her in our house. It was a sanctuary ideally suited to her, with a direct exit leading to our sprawling backyard, which stretched for an entire block. The sight brought a twinkle to her eyes, and I knew she had found her piece of paradise. As the days turned into weeks, Karla quickly settled into her new surroundings, embracing the vibrant energy of our neighborhood. We explored the nearby Italian market together, indulging in the delicious foods and cozy cafes. Karla's unique personality added light to our home; we treasured every moment spent together. Her presence and stories of her life with her late husband, Hans, brought an extra dose of joy to our lives.

Oh, how I miss my dear sister Karla and her wild antics. She may have been a rule-breaker, but she also brought me laughter and joy. So, here's to Karla, the unstoppable force of nature who danced to her own beat. May her spirit forever remind us to live with a dash of rebellion and a pinch of laughter. Cheers, sis!

60

A Battle Within

At the ripe old age of 80, I felt pretty good. But deep down, I couldn't help but feel a twinge of worry about what the future had in store for me. And Donna's depression only intensified my concerns. Who would take care of me if my health took a turn for the worse? Donna was already struggling to keep herself afloat. And my eighty-three-year-old sister, God bless her soul, began experiencing the dreadful onset of dementia.

So, we made a bold move and changed our lives completely. We packed our stuff and headed to Phoenixville, Pennsylvania, where my daughter Sabine lived. We found a beautiful house on an acre-and-a-half of land was a beauty there, but the real kicker was that it was just a ten-minute walk from Sabine, her fantastic husband Jordan, and our three adorable grandkids, Grace, Emery, and Ian.

The moment we stepped into our new house, a wave of pure happiness washed over us. It had this magical aura, as if giving us a big, warm hug. We knew we had made the right decision, and boy being so close to our daughter and grandkids brought us more joy than we imagined. We had spontaneous family get-togethers filled with laughter, love, and delicious meals. Our grandchildren would run around the vast backyard, their giggles echoing. It was pure bliss. And the people in Phoenixville were terrific. Our neighbors quickly became our friends, and we'd often gather for neighborhood cookouts or to chat. We felt like we truly belonged.

Life is a whirlwind of unexpected wonders, both delightful and challenging. And yes, occasionally, those challenges sneak up on the ones we hold dear. But when we settled into our vibrant new Phoenixville community, my heart was brimming with hope and excitement for Donna. I knew this fresh start would sprinkle her days with joy and endless positivity. Yet, despite our best wishes, her pesky depression persisted, casting a shadow on our otherwise sun-filled adventures. Despite my challenges, I couldn't help but feel a whirlwind of emotions. There were moments of frustration and confusion, wondering why Donna could not conquer her battles. But I tried to understand that everyone has their own journey. It was tough witnessing her constant attachment to her phone, detached from the world. Managing all the household tasks alone weighed on me, but I knew I had the strength to persevere.

In times of struggle, I found solace in writing. It became a creative outlet to pour out my emotions and find clarity. Still, I couldn't help but wonder why Donna seemed unable to lend a hand in our daily routines. From cooking meals to managing finances, everything overwhelmed her. It felt like she lacked the motivation to contribute, leaving me to take on all the responsibilities.

Despite these challenges, I remain hopeful, knowing that even in the most challenging times, there is a glimmer of brightness. I understand that everyone's journey with depression is different, and what may help one person might not be the right fit for another. I'm dedicated to providing practical support for her, whether by helping with chores or running errands. I've been a cheerleader for Donna to jump into daily tasks, reminding her it could sprinkle a little purpose and achievement into her life. Considering her feelings, boundaries, and dreams, I've been tackling this with all the sensitivity and understanding I can muster. Being there for Donna in her fight against depression has taught me the importance of really listening and understanding where she's coming from. Her happiness means the world to me, so I reassure her that her feelings are accurate and that I am here to support her.

Besides taking care of the usual household tasks, I gently nudged Donna to consider seeing a therapist or counselor. But she wants to handle it solo, and I understand and support her choice, even if I truly believe that seeking professional help could equip us with excellent tools and strategies to better navigate her condition.

I have also realized that self-care is necessary for both Donna and me! Being there for someone dealing with depression can be a roller coaster, so I've made it a priority to look after myself, too. I've reached out to my amazing friends and family, relying on their love and understanding as I vent my worries and share my experiences. It's been a fundamental change, giving me a safe space to recharge and keep my spirits high.

61

The Unforgettable Journey: A Tale of Love and Loss

During the tumultuous period of Karla's battle with dementia, life took an unexpected turn. Like a relentless storm, her condition deteriorated rapidly, causing confusion and disorientation. We knew we needed to transform our home to ensure her safety, so we began installing an array of safety features.

First was a chair lift to aid her in climbing the stairs. But our journey didn't end there. We understood the importance of adapting every aspect of Karla's life to her constantly growing needs. We elevated her bed, which allowed her to rise gracefully and effortlessly. We also installed motion and bed sensors, silent guardians that would alert us to her every move. If she wandered in the night, we could now lend a helping hand.

But one day, tragedy struck. A feeling, a whisper in the wind, tugged at my senses, urging me to hasten my steps. As I raced toward our house, fear clawed at my heart, and what awaited me inside was a sight I'll never forget. There, lying on the floor, was Karla, her face etched with pain and confusion. In a moment of misplaced bravery, she had attempted to ascend the stairs without the lift, but her frail body could not make it. She'd fallen.

Karla's condition became critical, and hospice care was our only choice. Our home became a sanctuary of compassion as we tended to her every need, enveloping her fragile spirit with love. But a week later, we took her to a hospice facility in Philadelphia's lovely Rittenhouse Square, to be with people who shared her struggle. I stood by her side, a steadfast guardian, refusing to let her face the darkness alone. Day and night blurred together as I held her hand, whispered words of love, and shared memories. On March 24, 2023, the world lost a shining light, and my heart shattered into a million pieces.

Karla's absence left a gap that was impossible to fill. Her laughter, kindness, and unwavering spirit—everything that made her unique—vanished from my life. My heart ached and I longed deeply for my cherished sister.

As I reflect upon our lives together, I cherish the moments of joy, the battles fought, and the unconditional love that bound us. Karla's legacy lives on in my heart, reminding me to embrace life's challenges with courage and to cherish each precious moment.

Before Karla's passing, she was excited about the upcoming spring season, with all its vibrant colors and rebirth, at our new home in Phoenixville. It brought me great sadness that she could not experience it. As the days grew longer and the weather warmed, our new home came alive with nature's wonders. The previously barren trees started growing delicate buds, showing lush greenery. The transformation would have captivated Karla as she marveled at the intricate details of every blooming flower and the fragrant scents in the air.

One late afternoon, as I sat in the backyard reminiscing about our shared memories, a gentle breeze carried the sweet fragrance of spring. It was as if nature was reminding me of Karla's presence and love for all the beautiful things. The chirping birds filled the atmosphere, their melodic songs harmonizing with the rustling leaves. It was a symphony that Karla would have cherished, her heart overflowing with joy and gratitude for life's simple pleasures. I could almost imagine her laughter blending with the music of nature, creating a soulful melody that danced through the air. Springtime in Phoenixville brought with it a delightful array of wildlife. The colorful butterflies moved gracefully between flowers, with wings painted in electric blues and fiery oranges. Karla's eyes would have glistened with childlike wonder as she watched their delicate dance. She would have spent hours in the garden, carefully tending to the blossoms and creating a sanctuary for these enchanting creatures. As the days turned into weeks, new life was imminent. The once-silent trees became bustling neighborhoods for birds, their nests housing precious eggs awaiting hatching. Karla's nurturing spirit would have been a beacon of warmth for these feathered families; she would have eagerly watched, marveling at the miracles of nature unfolding before her eyes.

One morning, as I strolled through our turtle pond area, I stumbled upon a nest tucked safely among the branches of a large bush. Carefully peering inside, I discovered a hatchling, its tiny beak opened wide, eagerly awaiting its first meal. It was a sight that would have undoubtedly brought tears of joy to Karla's eyes. Spring in our garden in Phoenixville was a melange of colors, scents, and sounds that would have awakened Karla's senses and filled her heart with boundless happiness. She would have relished in the beauty of each moment, cherishing the minor miracles surrounding us. Though she may not have been physically present to witness the magic of spring, her spirit lives on, forever intertwined with the essence of this season.

As I sit here, sharing Karla's story, my heart swells with sadness and gratitude. Sadness for the moments she has missed, but gratitude for the memories we created together and the love we shared. As spring unfolds, I find solace in the belief that Karla's spirit dances among the blossoms, forever a part of the eternal cycle of life and renewal.

62

The Final Chapter: Embracing Your Potential, Soaring to New Heights, and Unleashing the Power Within

As I sit here at eighty-two, reflecting on the journey that brought me to this point, I am overwhelmed with gratitude and a deep sense of purpose. Through the highs and lows, the triumphs and tribulations, I have realized that life is a beautiful medley of experiences that shape us in ways we could never imagine.

Life has a funny way of throwing obstacles in our path. It tests our resolve, pushes us to our breaking point, and sometimes knocks us down. But the accurate measure of our character lies not in how many times we fall but in how many times we rise again. I have learned that failure is not the end, but a stepping stone towards success.

Throughout my life, I have faced hardships that seemed impossible. From living through war to finding myself in refugee camps, I have had to start over and rebuild my life from nothing more times than I can count. And yet, through it all, I have emerged stronger, wiser, and more determined than ever.